WINGING IT

Also by Keith Spicer:

A SAMARITAN STATE? EXTERNAL AID IN CANADA'S FOREIGN
POLICY.

CHER PÉQUISTE . . . ET NÉANMOINS AMI.

WINGING IT

Everybody's Guide to Making Speeches Fly Without Notes

Keith Spicer

DOUBLEDAY & COMPANY, INC., GARDEN CITY, NEW YORK
DOUBLEDAY CANADA LIMITED, TORONTO, ONTARIO
1982

Library of Congress Cataloging in Publication Data

Spicer, Keith.
  Winging it.

  1. Public speaking. I. Title.
PN4121.S77   808.5′1
AACR2
ISBN 0-385-15764-9 (hard cover)
ISBN 0-385-18225-2 (paperback)
Library of Congress Catalog Card Number 80–8644

For Nick, Genevieve and Dag—
with love as they spread their wings.

Acknowledgments

First I wish to thank friends, acquaintances, and strangers who have told me they might buy, or at least furtively consult, a book such as this. Next I am grateful for the intelligent and sweet-tempered perfectionism of Gwenda Ellwood, who acted here as my typist but who writes her own stories with a natural grace. Then I thank two volunteer proofreaders, my friends Eileen Frank and Emmanuelle Gattuso, talented multi-media ladies to whom I owe many more Chinese dinners.

Finally, how can a writer thank his editors? Ritually, lukewarmly, or heartfeltly. With me it is truly the latter, for Ken McCormick and Mary Trone of Doubleday in New York, as well as Rick Archbold and Janet Turnbull of Doubleday Canada in Toronto, have treated me that kindly. All of them encouraged, and tactfully egged on. Janet Turnbull assumed the rigorous task of coordinating advice from New York and Toronto; she also guided my revisions with the judgment of Gertrude Stein, the zeal of a mother superior, and the gentleness of Irma la Douce. Mopping up of style and syntax, plus offering further pointers on how Canadians can make sense to Americans, fell to Mary Trone of Doubleday in New York, whose dedication to clarity I revere.

To one and all, bouquets. I'll take the brickbats and, if any, the royalties.

K. S.

Contents

Acknowledgments   vii

Introduction   xiii

Part One

UNDERSTANDING HOW: THE METHOD   1

**Chapter One: How a "Spontaneous" Speech Turns On
          Your Audience . . . and You**   3

    1. Your Captive Audience Is Captivated by . . . 4

    2. You, the Speaker, Can Take Off Beause You
      Can . . . 9

Chapter Two: A Tip-off Before Takeoff   19

    1. Demystifying Descartes 19

    2. Making Movies in Your Mind 23

    3. Salvation in Triplicate: Simplify, Illuminate,
      Advance 24

Chapter Three: The Three-Part Plan As Teleprompter   26

1. Why You Need a Plan 26

2. Why a Three-Part Plan Is Best 29

3. Why and How To Find a Core-Theme First 32

Chapter Four: Shaping a Compelling Plan   42

1. Breaking Down the Core-Theme 43

2. Letting Your Conclusion Choose the Plan 56

Chapter Five: Fleshing Out Your Plan   69

1. Filling In Your Three-Part Structure 69

2. Wrapping Up the Introduction and Ending 81

Part Two

MASTERING HOW: DRILLS AND DELIVERY   93

Chapter Six: From Drill to Instinct   95

1. Random Rehearsal 97

2. Scrounging for Topics 98

3. Nibbling to the Core 100

4. Instant Plans 106

5. Plan "Parties" 121

6. Stealing Practice 123

7. Volunteer Quickies 124

Chapter Seven: The Real McCoy   126

1. List Your Headings 127
2. Draft Your Opening and Closing 130
3. Dry Runs into Your Subconscious 137

Chapter Eight: Six Tricks for Takeoff   142

1. Infiltrate Your Audience 143
2. Psych Up, Offstage and On 148
3. Listen to Who You Are 151
4. Listen to Your Voice 157
5. Look at Your Audience 158
6. Roll the Credits 160

Chapter Nine: Twelve Ways Not To Crash   164

1. Underline Your Plan 165
2. Keep It Simple 169
3. Follow Fowler, etc. 171
4. Nail Down Each Point 173
5. Let Emotions Follow Thoughts 175
6. Use Humor Naturally 177
7. Exploit Slips, Blanks, and Malapropisms 179
8. Foresee and Finesse Hecklers 185
9. Appeal to Higher Instincts 190
10. Play the Applause 192

11. End on a Peak 198

12. Land on Time 199

Part Three

**DIGESTING WHEN AND WHY:
THE AERODYNAMICS OF ELOQUENCE 201**

Chapter Ten: When Not To Wing It   203

1. When Speaking for Posterity 206

2. When It's a Life-or-Death Issue 207

3. When Imprecise Language May Cost You
   Friends or Money 208

4. When You Want the Press To Quote You
   Accurately 210

5. When Your Talk Is a Laundry List 211

Chapter Eleven: Why (Again) and When To Fly   215

1. Written Speech Makes Rotten Speech 215

2. Practice Makes Fallibly Impressive 226

Chapter Twelve: Broodings After Touchdown   229

1. Eloquence in Eclipse 229

2. The Ironic Alchemy: Fighting TV's Fire with
   'Televised' "Thought on Fire" 238

The aim of . . . oratory is to teach, to delight, to move.

—CICERO

Introduction

Why are you buying, borrowing, or browsing this book? Because you suspect it could be fun and/or useful to speak in public without notes: to wing it.

It is. I've been winging it for more than twenty years, and I'm still amazed at how easily thinking on your feet can stimulate you, the speaker—while making your audience think you are brighter than you really are! This book teaches you a simple, reliable way to "improvise" speeches and spiels of all kinds for pleasure or profit. Let's see first why you will enjoy winging it, then how this technique will work for you.

What scares more people than cancer, flying, or loss of sex appeal? The world's most corrosive but curable social disease: shyness. A good way to cure shyness is by learning to speak in public without notes—by winging it. Incidentally, it's also the best way to salvage the nearly lost art of eloquence.

Shyness is the fear of looking silly. To stifle worries of

appearing to be out of style in clothes, food, movies, art, or music, we usually embrace an innocent enslavement to fashion. Shyness in speech hurts us more deeply. To shake it off, we must look for answers not in me-tooism but in something like I-don't-give-a-damn-ism.

Why does speech touch our feelings so poignantly? Because language most intimately echoes our dignity as human beings. Apart from feeling rejection in love, we suffer the cruelest humiliation from being unable to communicate our wishes, ideas, and emotions. How well we convey these thoughts and feelings shapes all our relationships: with family, friends, lovers, colleagues, and employers.

Whether these relationships are happy or destructive depends far more than we realize on our adroitness in expressing ourselves with accuracy and impact. This is true of table talk and of pillow talk. It is true of casual meetings and of rendezvous.

It is also true of formal meetings and presentations— of any communication which could roughly be called a "speech." Onstage freezing up, blank-minded terror, and inarticulate meandering shatter careers every day.

But doesn't the very idea of taking the floor without some paper crutch trigger such horrors? Only when you are unprepared: only when you don't know your subject or don't know how you plan to develop it.

A plan is, precisely, the key to winging it. The bedrock of winging it is a three-part outline which you work out carefully before your speech, then roll past your mind's eye while you are speaking. The idea of three-part outlines comes from a method of French logic loosely blamed on the seventeenth-century philosopher-mathematician René Descartes. The idea of "rolling" the outline past your mind's eye simply adapts to your imagination the concept behind a text-reading device used widely on TV—the teleprompter.

Think of winging it as Descartes on a teleprompter. If you can't stand French philosophers and don't like TV, think of it as running recipes on an invisible slide projector —or, more broadly, as just getting your act together and taking it on the road.

As Chapter One will spell out in detail, using this method will make you a far more controlled, self-assured speaker. It will focus your message, adding conviction and spontaneity. It will let you lead your audiences. As you come to see such results over months and years, you will wake up one day knowing the ecstasies of eloquence, knowing you have changed stage fright from enemy to ally.

You will hear much in this book about order freeing imagination, about structure being the gateway to liberty. As we fling you off the oratorical dock to sink or swim, you will quickly learn that the secret of killing terror, and of keeping afloat, is not to paddle frantically in all directions, but to stroke firmly in a *planned* direction.

If you relate better to art than to sport, think of Oscar Peterson studying Bach in order to become the world's greatest improviser of jazz piano. Think of Michelangelo's statue of David. Before he carved out its shape and spirit, it was just a dumb hunk of rock.

Who needs such fancy theory? Are not such issues and examples for the likes of Demosthenes and Cicero, Churchill and FDR?

No. They're stuff for anybody who needs to make a point, pass along information, peddle a product, or rally supporters—teachers, students, salespeople, executives, union leaders, politicians, professionals, preachers, prophets, Scout leaders, and con artists.

This book aims to help all such folk whose work or interests rely on persuasive speaking. It offers them a close-to-fail-safe formula for overcoming shyness when talking in public—and for improvising presentations that are clear, vivid, and memorable.

Many fine books teach you how to research, write, and deliver speeches. I think a lot of speakers would like to go a step further and train their minds—and nerves—to handle talks largely or wholly off-the-cuff. That's where *Winging It* fits on the bookshelf: as a method, which you can grasp in an afternoon and master in a month, for making well-focused, compelling statements to PTA, sales conference, annual meeting, church, or riot mob, completely without notes.

Can I guarantee you a standing ovation whenever you open your mouth? Maybe not. We all have off-days—even you and I and Demosthenes. But I've used the winging-it technique thousands of times in halls, amphitheaters, meeting rooms, and TV and radio studios for the past two decades, always keeping two or three steps ahead of lynching parties and tomato-throwers.

In speechmaking, as in life, the most prudent course is often calculated imprudence. The idea here is to take away the potential lynch mob's breath so that it has no wind left to chase you out of the hall. . . .

Read on, then. Part One will help you to understand

how winging it works; Part Two will tell you how to master it; and Part Three will aid you to digest some whys and wherefores, then fire you up to wing it soon and suavely. Read all this, then get ready to fire your speech writer, to throw away your crutches of prepared texts and idiot cards. Where your mind is going to fly you next time out, they will be excess baggage.

Bon voyage!
K. S.
Vancouver, B.C., May 1982.

Though practice in impromptu speaking is certainly useful, it is even more valuable to take time to consider what you are going to say.

—CICERO

It takes me three weeks to prepare a good impromptu speech.

—MARK TWAIN

Talking and eloquence are not the same: to speak, and to speak well, are two things. A fool may talk, but a wise man speaks.

—Ben Jonson

PART ONE

UNDERSTANDING HOW: THE METHOD

I grew intoxicated with my own eloquence.

—BENJAMIN DISRAELI

CHAPTER ONE

How a "Spontaneous" Speech Turns On Your Audience . . . and You

Before we plunge into the tricks of the impromptu trade, let's ponder where we are going. These first five chapters aim to help you understand winging it. They break down your flight toward eloquence into three phases: Chapter One tries to fuel your enthusiasm with reminders of the fun ahead; Chapter Two briefs you on the bare-bones technique of flying noteless; and the three final chapters spell out, step by step, how you can actually get airborne.

We'll begin by psyching you up to fly on. For both audience and speaker, a written speech is far less fun than a "winged" one. How, exactly, does the noteless talk work its magic? Let's do a little shrink-job first on your listeners, then see how you, the speaker, can fly high without a text for your ticket.

1. Your Captive Audience
Is Captivated by . . .

There is a whole range of impressions that will elicit, then sustain, your audience's attentiveness. Here they are:

a) *Your Knowledge:* The first reason any group of people decides to listen to you (discounting courtesy, boss's orders, or taking-your-turn protocol) is the presumption that you have something to say. After all, you are supposed to know more about the topic than they do.

If you recall half the speeches you have ever heard, you know that this supposition is a fragile one. More often than not, if you are listening to a colleague in molecular physics or Albanian pinochle, you know as much about the subject as he does—or you like to think so.

The notion of your superiority plants itself in listeners' minds first, of course, through the reputation that precedes you. You may have written a book (even one on public speaking can bring a flicker of fame); you may have won a prize, contest, or dizzying promotion, gone to jail, taught in a high-falutin' institute, run a cartel or a corporation; you may have launched a thousand ships with your face, or merely slain a dragon or two. In some way, big-league or bush-league, you come with ready-made credentials. These deliver you on a platter to your public as a certified celebrity.

If you can't trade on notoriety, chances are your host's introduction will pump up your balloon. Hosts need to prove they are smart hosts. That means hyping you as some sort of catch or coup. "We are privileged today," "It gives me great pleasure and honor," "Our distinguished speaker"—all this ritual claptrap may well apply in your case. Then again, it may not. The point is, your host must lay it on your listeners to give the whole occasion some class, or at least some vague sense of moment.

The moment is your momentum. A suitably fawning intro imprints you on the audience's mind as a person of weight. It should stir listeners awake, unplug their ears, and dispose them to give you a fighting chance to live up to your billing. However, neither reputation nor introduction can carry you far if, as soon as you open your mouth, you sound and look incompetent. This is where winging it or not stamps you as master or amateur. You may, in your field, be an Einstein or an Arnold Palmer; if you don't know your stuff well enough to explain it without notes, you mark yourself as a loser.

Rightly or wrongly, we judge people as speakers or performers by the apparent ease of their effort. We do this to Yehudi Menuhin, Linda Ronstadt, Billy Graham, and Hank Aaron. Toscanini's legend grew in part from conducting symphonies without a score.

Dragging notes onstage only telegraphs the idea that you had to make a big effort to bone up on your theme, then were so unsure of yourself that you had to sweat through a close read so as not to blow your lines. Appearing to improvise flashes you onto listeners' mind-screens as an authority, an expert. Playing the puppet by reading a text or clinging to notes takes you down, peg by peg, until you look even with, or even below, your audience.

Audiences are elitist. They want speakers to be better than they. As on TV, "visuals" go halfway toward convincing them; words and delivery do the rest. If you want to keep and deepen the authority-image you drew from your reputation and introduction, look authoritative. Wear your learning lightly. Prove that your expertise is really in your head, not just on pieces of paper your dimwitted cousin cribbed together from the public library. Fly solo, and prevail.

b) *Your Mental Discipline:* The terror of bombing in public is so universal that 90 percent of any audience (the really "unaccustomed to public speaking") look on any decent stump speaker as a practitioner of black magic. If you can play such a magician plausibly, you will pass—forgive me—for somebody even smarter than you are.

I'm not saying that by winging it, you can get away with a shoddy speech—but you can certainly get away with a speech which, if rattled off from the page, would seem pedestrian. Winging your talk enhances everything you say. It magnifies your magic, focuses your clarity, buttresses your logic. Not because you really are doing these things better, but because your stand-alone ability to think on your feet just makes everything you say sound more controlled and resourceful.

Much of this is pure illusion. But what is reality if not someone's perception of what *is?* What you are is what you appear to be doing: remembering and thinking without the prompting less gifted mortals need.

In the end, your arguments may still not sway your audience. They may be too partisan or rooted in their opposition to your ideas, or you may not have trotted out sufficient evidence to bring them around. What remains of even this "unsuccessful" effort is greater respect for you. And that means you can lie thee down, bleed a little, then rise to fight another day—with the assurance that you will get another crack at this stubborn gang.

c) *Your Emotional Control:* For nearly all of us, stage fright is natural. Even after long training and practice, we face any audience of more than half a dozen with a rise in blood pressure, from diffident little butterflies right up to blinding hysteria.

Again the act of standing up noteless (or even sitting down, seminar-style) before an audience works its magic. Your high-wire memory and moxie first stun your listeners. Then, as you get partway across with no net in sight, your boldness and control stir their astonishment.

High-wire daring is the right analogy: when you talk without a text, part of the thrill of watching you, and hearing you, lies in waiting for you to fall. Secretly, the audience hopes to see you fall, though not fatally. As with the Flying Wallendas, deep down the spectators want you to succeed, though with some fleeting proof of your fallibility —a slip, a pause, a split-second, salvaging grasp at the wire on the way down.

This excitement you fire by risking your reputation keeps your listeners awake, thus more open-eared to your spiel. It also builds into admiration which, as all but the neurotic know, initiates and underpins any healthy love. You crave affection with your triumph? Take balance-pole in hand, and tread gingerly but confidently.

d) *Your Unfolding Personality:* You are, as I am and we all are, a fascinating smorgasbord of hopes, fears, talents, hang-ups, virtues, vices, strengths, weaknesses, and contradictory values. Join the club. We are all eccentric.

One of the most savory pleasures of meeting new people is watching their personalities drop masks and veils. Your speech is an occasion for people to get to know you, or get to know you better. You should not disappoint them by overly scripting your self-revelation. Your nakedness (we are talking here of paper cover-ups, of course) is compelling, but your intellectual striptease is even more exciting.

No person can speak (or for that matter write) about any subject under the sun without telling a sensitive listener plenty about who the speaker is. Your data and arguments may echo the standard litany for defending your viewpoint. But your personal psychology, culture, thought processes, biases, and yardsticks add up to a trademark as intimate and unique as a fingerprint. When your words are written out and read, the joy and certainty of discovering the "real you" suffer: the stuff might very well have been ghosted by a Norwegian gnome.

To give your listeners the best show for their money, patience, and time, let them get to know you a little by letting go a little. Allow your words to fall into place, allow random but related thoughts to leap to your lips. Warts and all, stumbles and solecisms (if not insistent), your show-and-tell will engage your voyeuristic captives. With luck and practiced assurance, you will even charm them.

e) *The Integrated Power of Your Presentation:* We are flirting with seduction. Impressing your listeners with your knowledge, mental discipline, courage, and human richness adds up to an all-fronts assault on their credulity.

You need recoil from none of this because you suspect you lack brainpower or inborn charisma. Whatever you've got will look and sound better if you can train yourself to persuade without paper. As the song said, it's what you do with what you've got that matters. Once you are skilled in winging it, your audience will only cherish more whatever you say.

2. You, the Speaker, Can Take Off Because You Can . . .

Winging it helps you rev up yourself as well as your audience. How?

a) *Concentrate on Quality:* The quality of your facts, arguments, and style all rely on your paying attention to what you are saying. Too often the mechanics of reading (turning pages, flipping cards, lifting and lowering your head, finding the place where you left off) distract you more than they turn you on to your theme.

Paradoxically, reading can make you more nervous—and thus jerky, uptight, and stilted—than you would be as an orator well anchored in your ideas, but free to seek the natural rhythms of improvisation.

Noteless, you have literally nothing better (or worse)

to do up there onstage than focus on what you are saying and will say. You will be delighted to find that your grammar, imagery, and wit all come out more carefully wrought than they do in normal one-to-one speech. As we all are, you may tend to be sloppy, even a little slovenly, in street, home, or office speech. Onstage, with footlights real or metaphorical silhouetting you, you know you've got to perform.

In general, you will find that you can. Challenge makes charisma.

b) *Interact with Your Audience:* Again using the metaphor of seduction, remember that most of the pleasure in public speaking comes from building a relationship with your audience. If you are a whistle-stopping politician, you may tend to think of your audiences as an endless, and unrequiting, series of one-night stands. If you do, too bad. There are "meaningful relationships" to be savored even in brief encounters.

Always think of your speech as a two-way communication, a mutual exploration. If this simple little thought sounds too theoretical and preachy, recall the enchanting advice which Tallulah Bankhead gave the paramour to whom she slipped her apartment key: "If I'm not there by midnight, start without me."

You can't start or end a talk satisfyingly unless you plan to wrap your words around your listeners. Read their faces and noises, and try to mold your message to their needs. They will tell you as much about you as you are telling them about your subject. Listen, learn, and . . . liaise. Diplomats do; so can you.

c) *Cultivate a Sense of Theater:* The second you step behind the footlights—even if that means only sitting down at a meeting of five people—you become an actor. This is not such an exotic role. All of us, every day, unless we are mindless blabbermouths, act in front of others. We put on masks, fine-tune our voices to "performance" pitch, then prove Shakespeare right: "All the world's a stage, and all the men and women merely players."

Once we cross the border into formal communication, we need to heighten our art. We need to measure our public, its mood and outlook, its size, even lighting and acoustics. As these dictate, we must use gestures, pauses, tone of voice, and diction to sharpen the ideas and images we convey. Our cleverness in adapting our skills to the audience mirrors our sense of theater.

Make no mistake: matching your stage wiles to your public and the medium is of critical importance. Imagine the same message given in your five-person meeting, with close eye-contact, being broadcast on TV, or spoken to eight hundred people in a meeting hall.

You could translate much of your small-meeting technique to television, though you would do better in that most intimate of media by trying to charm the camera lens as a single listener. For the crowd of eight hundred, you would have to exaggerate diction, voice modulation (sharper contrasts for plainer separation of ideas), and, of course, gestures. If you used this big-crowd technique on closeup TV, it would look and sound inflated, if not phony. TV, indeed, because it unmasks and makes laughable the tub-thumpers of old-time religion and politics, has speeded the decline of good speech by confusing eloquence, in timid speakers' minds, with mere rhetoric.

To keep this distinction clear, and let you command your stage with the precise brand of eloquence your setting requires, you must escape the tyranny of notes. Since paper onstage takes on a meaning and law of its own, you must stay free of it to keep your stage skills in sync with your audience. It's not enough to say, "Ah, I'm facing twenty-five people in a semi-solemn forum, therefore I'll use technique number seven and just read on with my talk." You have to make such a judgment at the outset, of course. But to hold your stage and audience, you must be free to shift voice, gestures, even your body language.

Body language, you say? Yes. Call it stage presence and it won't sound so sinister. But study up on it and all the basic skills of speech (breathing, projection, voice control, diction), then use them joyfully without the distraction of taking your script onstage.

Aren't we getting a bit complicated for all those ordinary, day-to-day exchanges we get into? Maybe. But think how devastating Orson Welles was with pregnant pause and glance while assuring you that Paul Masson would never peddle you a caressing old burgundy . . . "before its time." With practice, you'll get an Academy Award for the way you ask about the weather.

d) *Surpass Yourself:* We spoke earlier of "creative terror." You get terror free of charge, as universal, old-fashioned stage fright. The creative element of fear must be learned. It refers to the clarity your thinking takes on when you harness terror.

This notion of fear leading to keener thought is not new. "Depend upon it, sir," assured Samuel Johnson in 1778, "when a man knows he is to be hanged in a fortnight, it concentrates his mind wonderfully." If you can get gutsy enough to wing your public persuasions, you will find that all the weapons in your oratorical arsenal grow sharper: not just clarity (mother of all stylistic virtues), but rhythm, imagery, nuance, and wit. You will, in short, rise above your text-proven talents. Your stomach may be sinking, but your head will be singing.

e) *Release and Channel Emotions:* I would not argue that all speakers who read texts or notes have sluggish digestion. But so many sound that way, don't you agree? Let's see how free speaking can make you sound and feel healthier.

Considering emotions experienced during periods of tension leads us to ponder the theory of stress. Dr. Hans Selye, of McGill University in Montreal, pioneered a theory with this premise: when faced with a sudden challenge, your body and psyche can either resist or adapt, fight the stress or embrace it. If your body systems judge that they can overcome the stress, they will fight it; if they "reason" it is too strong, they accept it—and, in doing so, sap its destructiveness.

When you read a speech or rely heavily on notes, you are admitting that the stress that stages, audiences, and microphones cause is insurmountable. Yet you are fighting it fatalistically and, for the vigor of your speech, perhaps fatally. You are allowing stress to paralyze your thinking, to cripple your reasoning, possibly even to stiffen your body language. Your crutch to cope with this paralysis is, of course, your text—and every time you shuffle a page or a card you remind yourself that you are handicapped.

When you dare to speak noteless, you are accepting the inevitable stress as conquerable. You are trying to beat it the way a judo expert of small stature overcomes a hulking opponent: you use the adversary's own weight against him. The secret with the big brute on the judo mat is to think of his weight as a potential ally. The same goes for that knot in your stomach: if you think of it not as a threatening dead weight but as a miniature nuclear reactor, a ball of energy, you can turn it to astounding effect. You can master the negative tension by channeling it as a positive force.

By changing fear into hope, you change the whole chemistry of stage fright. You begin to welcome back the butterflies, by telling yourself you need their tender tickling in your tummy to keep you in peak form.

That last thought, I assure you, is the common wisdom of nearly every great stage performer. Ask the coolest ballerina or sword-swallower of your acquaintance if she or he likes to be totally relaxed when performing. Reasonably relaxed, they'll say, but just on edge enough to avoid a careless pratfall or sliced esophagus.

All of this chatter of stress psychology leads you to what, in practice? If you turn the tables on terror, you'll no longer sound sluggish. You will open up the sluice gates of *constructive* emotion, of felt, spontaneous, juicy, loving-or-angry-but-credible caring. You'll help your heart fuel your mind. You'll put lead in your pencil, a tiger in your tank, a sizzle on your steak, a fire in your furnace. You'll make a friend of fear, and a speaker of you. When, now, will you stir us with your next three-hanky movie?

f) *Rediscover Your Subject:* All this high-wattage candlepower you've got going for you brings light as well as heat: it illuminates your topic. More precisely, it turns on a searchlight that reveals new paths, new byways off the highways of your conscious knowledge.

Once you get the hang of thinking on your feet, you will find that the thrill of risk-taking infects your imagination with wanderlust. Instead of being trapped inside the pre-programmed itinerary of a text, you are free to roam into new vistas on your old theme. You will happen onto undreamed-of clearings and dells, whimsical digressions that heighten your freshness, sudden and quite often profound analogies, vivid new images, unclichéd wording, examples to quicken the spirit or trigger understanding.

Undreamed-of clearings and dells? At least I'm not promising you the soaring uplands of the soul. Just try to share, as examples, the following little en-route surprises.

Let's say you're a real-estate agent peddling condos in Hawaii. You start your standard profit-in-paradise spiel, straining not to scare off mainlander marks with fears that another Volcker-type freeze on credit could burst the whole damn condo market like the South Sea Bubble.

As you recite your litany in front of the credulous *haole* (that's Hawaiian slang for bleach-skinned continentals), you wander in orderly fashion through interest rates, leverage, and resale outlook. Then you discuss the impact of costlier aviation fuel on marketing. Your mind flashes to the deep-buried nugget you read two months ago in *Barron's*, announcing how gas from guano (Peruvian bird droppings) is going to bring OPEC to its knees and drive down oil prices. Click: *in guano veritas*. You instantly weave into your scam the diverting thought that more than one kind of manna falls from the skies. And because this manna is literally a gas, the planes from L.A. to Honolulu will continue to jet in Boeings full of buyers. If the marks believe that a bunch of birds are going to give us cheaper airfares, they'll believe all the poetry you purvey about interest rates.

A less malodorous example: this time you are a doctor, explaining to a group of patients why Medicare is bad for health—especially doctors' fiscal health. You trundle them through the thickets of the doctor-patient relationship, case loads, and quality of care. Then, on your way to the Forum, a funny thing happens: you suddenly remember the old merchandising maxim about low-cost, high-volume profits. An altruist to the marrow, you note that yours is the only free-enterprise profession in which mass-production millionaires can actually kill people. With Hippocrates and hypocrisy hand in hand, you hammer home your message that doctors are a class act, and must be allowed a few class privileges—such as fee-splitting and tax-dodging.

As you will see when we get into the winging-it technique, much of what passes for spontaneity can and should be thought out beforehand. The method taught here rests on the belief that discipline leads to freedom. First you build structure, then you fly confidently within it—confidently because you know that the structure is waiting to catch you as a safety net.

The most marvelous payoff of winging your talks is not so much in enriching your style. It lies in thinking out your subject afresh—thinking it out under the stimulating glare of metaphorical footlights. Scientists claim we rarely use more than one-seventh of our brain. When you take your chances onstage, you escape from such lazy thinking. You draw on your adrenaline and send it upstairs to spur on your brain, to get those billions of on-the-shelf gray cells to work for you.

I've found this process so challenging that I've sometimes ended a speech realizing that my "truths" were shakier than I'd thought. Putting them under bright-lights scrutiny in front of skeptical strangers forced me to reassess perspectives and priorities.

Being as slippery as the next guy, I would never admit this *during* a speech. But after a speech I've often realized that some kind of stage-triggered marination was occurring. Quietly, usually imperceptibly, analyzing my thoughts in interplay with the audience led me to rethink my message.

True believers beware: your ideas may not leave the stage in the same shape they went on in. Such a fate may leave you dangling like that last preposition.

g) *Strike a Mood of Seduction:* If making a pitch is a seduction, you might view all this as psychological foreplay. That's the idea—and it's catching. As in the unpublic dialogue of love, one partner's enthusiasm, like musk, awakens the other's. Learn to let loose. You will find that your collective partner in seduction, your audience, turns on with you almost nuance by nuance.

What more can I plead? If you don't bite on bait like that, maybe you should read more Gothic novels.

Now to work—and, if you don't have a headache, the technique of making love in full flight.

Our life is frittered away by detail. . . . Simplify, simplify.

—THOREAU

CHAPTER TWO

A Tip-off Before Takeoff

Before the nuts and bolts, the nutshell. Would you like to know in a few paragraphs just what you're letting yourself in for?

Okay. As we hinted in the Introduction, the essence of winging it is a marriage of two notions far apart in time and origin: Descartes wed to the teleprompter. If you find it comfier to think of this as rolling recipes upward on an invisible screen, fine. You've got the idea.

Let's take an advance peek at Descartes and his recipes, next see what a teleprompter does, then explain how they work together.

1. Demystifying Descartes

Descartes here is *not* the guy who played left wing for the Montreal Canadiens in 1923. We mean *René* Descartes

—the seventeenth-century favorite of Queen Christina of Sweden and author of the epoch-making book on clear reasoning called *Discourse on Method.*

Descartes, more than anyone, was the guy who taught Frenchmen to think—and to be insufferably arrogant forever after. It is not so much Descartes's own conclusions that matter to us now. His "I think, therefore I am" has given way to "I am all mixed up, therefore I can't really tell you whether or not I am or, if I am anybody at all, who the hell that somebody might be."

The modern tradition of Cartesian thought in France has been marked by systematic doubt cut and dried into a rigorous, very often three-part, formality. This approach to thinking is taught in French high schools and universities as an orthodoxy defying quarrel or quibble. It stands as the bulwark and very architecture of French reason. And, as you will soon agree, it offends ferociously the Anglo-Saxon psyche, which Frenchmen regard as hopelessly mired in fuzzy thinking and formless muddle.

The chapters immediately following will give you a cram course in what Frenchmen broadly call Cartesian method—a way of reasoning which we here update, adapt, and illustrate to fit a North American or British audience.

This "French" way of reasoning will save you enormous time, grief, and confusion. When you get the hang of it, it will get you adroitly through speeches of any length to any audience.

All you need to know for now is that *the three-part "Cartesian" plans or outlines on which you will learn to base your speeches are the secret of "spontaneous" speech-*

making. They force you to cut quickly to the core of any subject; they make you organize your topic into sections that flow logically into one another; and they help you remember your facts and arguments. Not least, they free you from fretting over the flight-plan of your thinking, so you can enjoy exploring your topic to its destination.

In short, our friend Descartes—or what now passes for Cartesian reasoning—allows you to lead your listeners clearly and confidently to your conclusions. It enables you to make speeches which audiences may not always agree with, but which they will understand, respect, and remember.

If you want to check out what Descartes said, take a look at Discourse 2 in his *Discourse on Method*. This short section spells out his way of reasoning in four "rules." You can sum these up as:

Rule 1: *filtering facts* (Descartes called this skeptical refinement of reality "intuition");

Rule 2: *breaking down the facts* into several simple, logical, or "solvable" parts (we'll call this analysis);

Rule 3: *reordering the facts* (and your evolving arguments) into a simple-to-complex pattern, by which you prove the easy things first through Rule 1's filtering skepticism (call this synthesis); and

Rule 4: *linking first principles to their end results* (call this deduction). For Descartes this was a key to both avoiding memory defects and keeping the whole argument on track to its conclusion.

Intuition, analysis, synthesis, deduction.[1] Descartes truly thought this method would make him the Aristotle of his era. He thought it could prove with mathematical certainty anything from a principle of physics to the existence of a Vatican-certified God.

That was, of course, before Sir Isaac Newton and Voltaire. Within a few years, Descartes's method, as a universal tool, lay in ruins—yet the issues he dealt with and the spirit of his inquiry lived on. As his recent British translator, F. E. Sutcliffe, put it: "If the system of Descartes was a failure, Cartesianism as an attitude was both fruitful and enduring."

You will see that winging it draws to some degree on all of Descartes's rules, but mainly it follows the Cartesian spirit: skeptical orderliness, geared to clarity as the supreme virtue. We are not dabbling here in seventeenth-century philosophy. That's why I refer to French thought and

1. In Descartes's own words:
"The first [rule] was never to accept anything as true that I did not know to be evidently so: that is to say, carefully to avoid precipitancy and prejudice, and to include in my judgments nothing more than what presented itself so clearly and so distinctly to my mind that I might have no occasion to place it in doubt.

"The second, to divide each of the difficulties that I was examining into as many parts as might be possible and necessary in order best to solve it.

"The third, to conduct my thoughts in an orderly way, beginning with the simplest objects and the easiest to know, in order to climb gradually, as by degrees, as far as the knowledge of the most complex, and even supposing some order among those objects which do not precede each other naturally.

"And the last, everywhere to make such complete enumerations and such general reviews that I should be sure to have omitted nothing."

winging it as being only broadly or loosely Cartesian. "Descartes" in this book is merely my shorthand for the French mindcast.

So before you announce yourself to the world as a modern Cartesian, remember: you're not parading as a disciple of post-medieval mathematics—just as a clear-headed genius.

2. Making Movies in Your Mind

The other spouse in this cross-cultural shotgun wedding is, as stated, the teleprompter. This clever device, in case you have never seen one, runs news bulletins past Dan Rather and other television luminaries who appear to improvise fifteen minutes of devilishly complex foreign and domestic happenings every night. You know: they never miss a syllable of "Baluchistan" or "Multiple Independently Targeted Re-entry Vehicles." As they roll all these tongue-twisting esoterica off their tongues with not a note in sight, you wonder whether *you* could get up in front of a TV camera and recall your name.

Teleprompters or variants on them are the rich person's (or well-paid professional's) electronic idiot cards: they carry the full text of a speech, bulletin, or commentary on a mirror in front of the TV camera lens. At the speaker's talking speed, a technician runs the text past the performer's eyes—but away from the audience's eyes.

On TV you see nothing except (if you're looking for it) the reader's eyes staring slightly above or below your own; when a major political or business figure makes a speech to a huge crowd, you sometimes spot funny-looking pieces of glass around his podium.

What you are going to learn in the next few chapters is the theory, method, and drill of a memory-speaking system which puts Descartes on the teleprompter. You will learn how to reduce any and every question to a core issue developed through a logical Cartesian-type plan; then you will learn to project your plan on an imaginary teleprompter focusing forward from the back of your head; finally, you will learn to roll your mind's-eye teleprompter, with bright, readable images, over the "picture" of your audience. This you will do at a speed that is steady but which varies to fit the speech's changing mood and opportunities for effect.

3. Salvation in Triplicate: Simplify, Illuminate, Advance

Do you want that in plain, containerized English? Memorize this three-part formula, then, and put it on your permanent mind's-eye teleprompter: *simplify, illuminate, advance*. Or, as you will learn to line up your imaginary recipe cards when speaking:

- Simplify.
- Illuminate.
- Advance.

Whenever you face a new topic, that is the procedure you will follow. If you take these steps in sequence, you will find that the most complex subjects lose their terrors and come clear. You will carve your way through the fog that shrouds the unfamiliar theme, and find that for your special audience there is a kernel or core of truth that really matters. Then you will identify three, four, or more ways of breaking down that core into sensible segments—which you can reassemble in the aptest way to prove your point. Finally, you will learn to turn up the lighting contrast on that TV screen in your brain to "see" the headings for your segments at will.

With the understanding gleaned in the next three chapters and the drills in Part Two, you will make winging it your instant, automatic, instinctive way of getting to the bottom of any subject. You will use it to reshuffle scattered ideas into a graspable, convincing pattern. Then, as you flash this pattern onto your secret mind-screen, you will speak splendid sense—or, at the very least, plausible nonsense.

Enough teasers. It's time for the fun. Throw away your Valium and idiot cards, and prepare to lose your fear of flying. Or, we might say, get ready to learn the joys of purposeful stage fright. Turn the page. It's a cinch.

I found that you could improvise all you wanted if you had a strong structure.

—Martin Cruz Smith,
author of *Gorky Park,* explaining how he learned to write by listening to his jazz-musician parents, cited in *Time* magazine

CHAPTER THREE

The Three-Part Plan As Teleprompter

Now, finally, the guts, the system—the rock-bottom, nuts-and-bolts secret of winging it: your plan. Before zeroing in on the finer points of plan plumbing, let's get three ideas straight: why you need a plan; why a three-part plan is best; and why and how to find a core-theme first.

1. Why You Need a Plan

You can know your subject cold. You can seethe with enthusiasm. You can sense soul-unity with your audience.

But if you cannot shape your eloquence, channel it, focus it into a skeleton of at least spurious logic, you will offer not a menu of ideas but a smorgasbord. And smorgasbords, far more often than planned menus, cause indigestion.

We non-French—whether of Chinese, Scandinavian, or especially English or American origin—fight desperately against shaping our eloquence. All our muddle-through, free-associating instincts drive us to believe that organizing our thoughts, and marshaling them for orderly presentation, somehow offends against our freedom of speech.

Left to our intuitive devices, we prefer to waffle. We love to plunge in anywhere on our discourse, meander along with barely a clock as our guide, then trail off aimlessly when we run out of steam or the audience runs out of cough drops.

The key to clarity, however—the secret of impact, punch, and bring-down-the-rafters stump speaking—lies in a sinful and frightfully un-English concept called form. Form—a premeditated, cunningly carved structure—is the magic formula for inspired "improvisation."

No doubt a silver-tongued few among us can pull off a truly spur-of-the-moment speech that does sing and move. But even good stump speakers can manage this only when in top spirits, and when dealing with a well-broken-in topic, an indulgent audience (old friends, cronies, peers), and a short, undemanding time allotment. The five-minute testimonial, with grins and gold watches, for an old colleague leaving the firm does not call for the same strong mind, stomach, and skills as does a sixty-minute technical extravaganza on the company's annual report or (for lawyers) on the accused embezzler's incandescent innocence.

The rest of us, the poor suckers who quail at asking permission to visit the bathroom during a routine meeting of the Harper Valley P.T.A., must find a crutch. We must reassure our timid tongue with a safety net, forearming our trembling ego with an outline of what we really want to say.

Let's knock away most of the traditional oratorical crutches—flip cards, point-form notes, or random paragraphs—as distracting and stylistically jerky. The prop we must learn to use for winging it is an embarrassingly simple new habit of thinking: the habit of thinking through each topic within a tailored-to-measure, inexorably plausible plan.

One last bit of hokum to psyche you up as a fanatic of form. If you already rebel at a system so obviously constipated as to rest on order, draw up your own list of geniuses whose unchained creative passion can be traced to an earlier mastery of their métier's classical disciplines. Start with Bach, Mozart, Beethoven; move on to Shakespeare, Molière, Einstein, Bobby Orr, and O. J. Simpson. You will find comfort with the "constipated"—virtually none of the biggies in anything turns out to be an "unstructured" virtuoso.

In mastering the trade of talk, you will find yourself in classy company. Hell, even Demosthenes trained with pebbles in his mouth.

2. Why a Three-Part Plan Is Best

A man I once met in a mental asylum (I think I was just visiting) told me: "You don't have to be crazy to be in here, but it helps if you are." And you don't have to cook up a three-part plan for every occasion you open your mouth, but I assure you it helps a great deal.

Why?

First, because three parts are numerous enough to display your talent for analysis—your ability to break down a topic into sections that you can at least make *appear* to hang together.

Second, if you reach beyond three parts (four in a pinch), chances are you have missed the core point of your topic. You cannot begin by telling an audience, "In outlining my views on birth control for armadillos, I'm going to identify thirteen major perspectives on the subject." By the time you get to the sixth or seventh perspective on this intriguing theme, you may be sure your entire audience will have goofed off to the zoo to figure out their own, far simpler, perspectives on armadillos.

Third, even before losing your audience you are likely to lose yourself. Wild as I am about armadillos personally, I'll be damned if I could remember more than three really poignant facts about them.

Fourth, in the annals of logic there stands a pretty durable tradition of three-part breakdowns. Aristotle's *Organon* treatises laid out a system of "syllogistic logic," based on two premises and a conclusion, which dominated Western reasoning for two thousand years. Example: Billy Carter grew peanuts; Billy Carter drank beer; possibly, just conceivably, therefore, beer goes well with peanuts.

Actually that's stretching the point a bit, because the peanuts need to be salted. But you get the idea.

Another three-part way of thinking with real internal combustion is Hegel's dialectic. This prodigiously pompous philosopher from Stuttgart (born 1770 and still alive, at least in communist countries) devised a charming little Ping-Pong game called thesis-antithesis-synthesis. In the kind of chitchat you and I indulge in, this could lead to something like: Billy Carter loved beer; Ruth Carter Stapleton loved the Bible; Jimmy Carter, with a foot in both camps, taught Sunday school but would occasionally sneak a sip of rather dry California chablis.

Speaking of communists, which we weren't really, Marx and Engels adapted Hegel to their economic theories to invent a three-part jaw-breaker called dialectical materialism. This, for the two billion human beings living in countries shaped by Marxist teachings, offers a method of solving problems by identifying contradictions—the struggle of opposites—which force unstoppable movement to new realities.

If ever you get in an argument with a well-schooled communist, you will understand how this mix-black-with-white-you-get-gray logic leads to dogmatism about the inexorable river of history, as well as just plain bull-headedness.

As a surface ploy, however, it carries undeniable power, even though its conclusions often make you yearn for the gentler days of Aristotle. Example: Jimmy Carter used to own the peanut warehouse in Plains; then Billy ran it as a blind trust for Jimmy; if they both had not been careful, Bert Lance might have foreclosed on the thing, left the National Bank of Georgia, and run the warehouse with juicy jobs for all his relatives.

All of that, you can see, proves something. At the very least it shows that the old three-part magic runs back a long way and can be mobilized, one way or another, to give a patina of logic to almost any argument.

A final plea for three-part advocacy rests—do not laugh—on the sheer irrational symbolism of the trilogy. Scour history, literature, art, music: you will spot a thousand instances where the human mind has sought symmetry in the mystery of threes. The Holy Trinity is just the best advertised of them all, and its power derives greatly from its avowed inscrutability. The same religious flavor attaches to faith, hope, and charity, the Three Wise Men, and "before the cock crows thrice." The Three Graces enchanted the ancients, Caesar divided Gaul into three parts, Aesop and Lafontaine peopled their fables with threes (the miller, his son, and the donkey), and the Three Stooges tickled us before even Jimmy, Billy, and Bert.

All in all, a three-part presentation, whether sermon, used-car pitch, lecture, or political stemwinder, can make you sound as though you actually know what you're talking about.

The trinity trick may sometimes strike you as strained. But your audience—if you highlight the plan, yet smooth its transitions, as we shall show—will sense the presence of an orderly mind. Such a mind offers its own three rare qualities: clarity, coherence, and logic. An illusion? Don't be so modest.

3. Why and How To Find
a Core-Theme First

Even before you dazzle your audience with your three-part plan, you must trot out proof of an orderly mind by giving a wise and lucid definition of your topic. Right off the top, you have to reach to the core issue most likely to grip your audience. To start any speech with authority, the heart of the matter is . . . the heart of the matter.

Why? Because to convince your listeners you know what you're talking about, you have to *know* what you're talking about. Insultingly obvious? Just ask yourself how many times you have left a speech, a presentation, a lecture, a debate, with the uneasy feeling that you could not guarantee what the topic truly was supposed to be.

According to your outlook and interests, most topics offer more than one possible "core." The idea is to choose one containing the issue that *you* know best or feel most strongly about, and which best fits the *audience's* known interests.

This choice of a core-theme should take a lot of your time (anything up to an hour at one thinking-blitz), for once you latch onto the core you are stuck with it. The vigor of your plan and delivery, and thus the impact of your speech, will both hang on how sound or flimsy a choice you make.

a) *Example 1: A Friendly Audience of Peers:* Let's get down to brass tacks. You are an insurance executive in Blowhard, Arizona, and you've got to recaptivate a captive audience of your peers at a statewide convention. The conference organizers dump on you a typically fuzzy grab-bag topic called "Insurance and our American Freedoms."

You flinch at the topic's vagueness. You are haunted by visions of yourself trapped into a John Wayne-Billy Graham flag-waver. You fear you'll have to rely mainly on heart-tugging rhetoric, instead of on the clear-headed, challenging analysis you would like to hear if you were in the audience.

You can still do a two- or three-handkerchief speech (for tears of patriotic emotion), but one which will be clear, focused—and, why not?—reprintable. How? By digging deep into the topic for an issue which you can honestly get worked up about, and which you think you can treat to meet the mentality, experience, hopes, and fears of your listeners.

What's the best way to decide that you and your audience could make beautiful music together? Take a piece of paper and give yourself twenty minutes. Then jot down in that time as many core-themes as you can that look like points where you and your audience might rendezvous.

If you concentrate on giving yourself and your imagined audience an intensive "brain scan," you will find that ideas flow fairly easily. Put these all down, no matter how off-base or far-out they seem at first. If they emerge from a solid knowledge of your audience, several ideas will probably look good as core-themes. Those you can't use as a core-theme may still come in handy as sub-themes or examples.

What happens if, after twenty minutes, the juices do not flow? You take off for a short coffee- and/or cognac-break. Fortified, you let the data in your "brain scanner" marinate a little longer, then you return to the task for another twenty-minute brainstormer. This time, or on the third or fourth try (especially with cognac) the juices will flow, or at the very least dribble intriguingly.

Let's look for a moment at your first piece of paper. On it you've tried to list possible core-themes by running a "scan" on yourself and your audience:

Core-Theme Search Through
Speaker-Audience Match-Up

Area: Insurance and Freedom

Speaker:

- 13 years in insurance, all kinds
- career goals: —start *own agency* specializing in fire and accidents
  —become president of Arizona insurance underwriters
  —run for state *politics* in three years
- insurance gave you and family financial independence (*self-reliance theme?*)
- multi-billion-dollar pool of policyholders' money gives America economic *stability, prosperity,* jobs, *freedom of choice* in enterprise

● worries: —*anti-business* *mystique* may in long run sap civil liberties
—*distrust of insurance firms* destroying huge investment pools

Audience:

● all insurance *professionals* (plus spouses aware of insurance)

● very *solid-virtue,* middle-class, mainly *small-town* folk

● hopes: —to see insurance industry prosper in wealth and *public acceptance*
—to own and run *independent* agency with *little government* or big-company interference

● fears: —that upcoming state law will *stifle small agencies* in effort to curb big firms
—that press and young people portray insurance people as *parasites*
—that intensifying *specialization* will make small all-purpose agencies obsolete

Out of this match-up of interests between you and your listeners you could spot a number of exploitable core-themes, all linking the issue of civil freedoms to the insurance industry:

POSSIBLE CORE-THEMES

(*Insurance and Freedom*)

- *Small is beautiful:* Self-reliant small-business owners, standing outside big government, big unions, and big business, are democracy's foot soldiers.
- *Liberty depends on stability:* The stable, prosperous society insurance helps create offers the necessary climate for civil liberties (instability=fear=intolerance).
- *Lobbies keep the public alert to freedoms:* Free associations have a duty to inform citizens of viewpoints differing from prevailing orthodoxies.

Once you identify two or three plausible core-themes, you have to nail one down, or even combine two into one by further refinement. In doing this you should be quick to spot themes you can sum up in an actual title (if you are allowed to tinker with this) or subtitle (which you can always invent, even if you just use it orally to focus your audience's attention).

For the first core-theme, E. F. Schumacher's "small is beautiful" would do fine. Since this time you are preaching to the deeply converted, you might even play around (straight-faced, one hopes) with "Insurance People: Democracy's Foot Soldiers." Personally I would lay off this kind of hype, even among the converted. If you have any hope at all of slipping your wisdom into the press, you can't have the reporters' pencils and TV cameras shaking too much from journalists' giggles.

The second core-theme might fly with something like: "Insuring Freedom Through Stability." Another possibility, recycling Franklin D. Roosevelt's phrase, would be "Freedom from Fear—Insurance and F.D.R.'s Fourth Freedom."

The third possible core-theme lends itself nicely to a link between selfish interest and civic duty—always a seductive thought to economic classes on a guilt-trip. "The Insurance Story—Why America Needs to Hear It As It Is" carries an appealing insinuation that the press, or somebody, has been telling the insurance story as it is not. It also hints at an aggressiveness which, as every cub reporter knows, may mean a good fight, a good headline, and an even better by-line.

If you think the traffic (i.e., your audience's sense of humor) will bear it, you might try a more whimsical theme-title, such as "Organizing to Tell the Insurance Story—There's Safety in Numbers."

You must commit all of these goodies to paper, look at them, brood on them. Then, after some disciplined dithering, you must make up your mind. Take one core-theme, roll it around in your mind and mouth until you really believe it's a winner, then move on to the next delights of winging it in Chapter Four.

b) *Example II: A Hostile Audience:* But before we get to dissecting a core-theme, let's do one more scanning expedition just for practice.

This time you're a teacher pleading with a group of Proposition 13 tax-cutting parents to reinstate a program of remedial reading for teenagers. Since you don't have to tell your life story to yourself every time you set out to focus on an audience, you may often prefer just to jot down your areas of expertise, not ambitions. Reminding yourself of your own background knowledge (including experience, reading, and documents at hand) can prove a sneaky way of sticking to core-themes you can readily research—a good work-saver as well as a guarantee that you will sound authoritative, possibly even enthusiastic.

CORE-THEME SEARCH THROUGH SPEAKER-AUDIENCE MATCH-UP

Area: Need for Remedial Reading

(*Trigger-words for core-themes are italicized*)

Speaker:

- *history* specialist with eight years' experience, including three in *guidance*

- concern: many bright kids are slowed down by sloppy reading skills; less bright ones are *sabotaged* and drop out: *waste* of talent

- belief: systematic reading skills can be taught quickly and cheaply; *cost-benefit* ratio excellent for entire curriculum; *all subjects are filtered* through reading ability

Audience:

- relatively *uneducated* parents

- fears: —*angry* at *rising taxes* and striking, "well-paid" teachers (sense of *rip-off*)

> —eager for children to stick to *basics, not "frills"* (like remedial reading?)
>
> ● hopes: —children will get *solid general* education
>   —get more *mileage* from tax dollar

This time the match-up of concerns between speaker and audience is plain: you, the teacher, and they, the parents, both deplore waste. You as a professional see mainly the squandering of young minds handicapped by feeble reading skills. They as taxpayers see escalating tax bills, fancy-carpeted schools, and apparently lousy teachers.

The way to reach your listeners? Show them—with figures on failure and drop-out rates—how classes of poor readers waste far more money (and still more precious hope) than do classes of good readers. You sell them remedial reading in the language of their own concerns: value for money. It's crass, but it's real; and for the kids who will profit from better reading, it's a bargain.

Your core-theme, if you want to seize your listeners by both pocketbook and heart, must obviously settle on a mixture of money and idealism:

POSSIBLE CORE-THEMES

(*Remedial Reading*)

Since the margin of choice here is narrow, you could jump straight to title-making to sharpen the topic more quickly:

- *Better Reading—Opportunity Is a Bargain:* disarmingly mercenary, but for this audience of Archie Bunkers, who see red (though not necessarily rednecks), that's likely what you need to pry their ears for your noble message.
- *Give Your Child a Chance—and Yourself a Break:* a scarcely more subtle trade-off between your listeners' hopes for their kids and fears for their holiday on Waikiki.
- *Opening All the Doors to Your Children:* if you sense parental love and pride are strong enough to carry you along the high road of idealism only, you could press the remedial reading case on its sole pedagogical merits. Then, at the end, if you still catch shadows of doubt flickering across a face or two, you could always tack on the cost-benefit "bargain" angle as a clincher. One of the joys of winging it is the chance to switch gears en route.

Both the above technique and the two examples need to be read with a chunky grain of salt. Like any method, they should be taken as guidelines or indicators, not as a system to follow slavishly. As you gain experience, speed, and discipline in leaping to the core of your subject, you won't need the routine of reminding yourself on paper of what your own interests and background are. These will intervene spontaneously as you stomp around the terrain to be explored.

The part you cannot skip is the "scan" of your audience. If you don't get a clear fix on your listeners' mental and professional background, on their hopes and fears in relation to whatever you might be able to tell them, you will lead a cavalry charge into a swamp.

One time you will find it easy to scrap a written match-up of you and the audience is when you know a fairly broad subject-area extremely well. Then you will probably face only the fun of sifting through your storehouse of expertise to fish out a core-theme tailor-made for each audience.

You may be a doctor specializing in natural childbirth. Your basic data remain the same for everybody, but for mothers, fathers, nurses, or Blue Cross administrators you must seek out a precise core-theme that meets the deepest cares and familiar symbolisms of the target group.

The real joy in doing the "rubber chicken" circuit (the speakers' tour of service clubs offering lunches of peas, potatoes, and badly cooked fowl) comes in scanning the audience beforehand, sizing up its mind and emotions, and trying to lock onto its idiom. For that is what a good speech should aim for: a clear, riveting translation of your ideas into your listeners' language, and thus into their consciousness.

That's why getting your core-theme right is the core concern. Finding your audience really means first finding for each group the issue that is most vital, exploitable, and —forgive that stale word—meaningful.

Next: how to cut cloth for a three-piece suit.

Speech finely framed delighteth the ears.

—The Bible, Apocrypha, Second Book of the
Maccabees

He liberates inner freedom in his actors, but at the
same time he frames them. There is simultaneous
freedom and control.

—Polish theater director Tadeusz Lomnicki,
assessing Roman Polanski's Warsaw debut in
Amadeus (New York *Times,* July 21, 1981)

CHAPTER FOUR

Shaping a Compelling Plan

First, a word from your sponsor. A three-part plan as we
mean it here has nothing to do with the three-part essay
form that Miss Grumpypuss, your old high-school teacher,
taught you: introduction, body, conclusion. Miss Grumpy-
puss, God bless her, was drilling you in literary analysis.
This book aims to teach you noteless public speaking: how
to get ideas out of your head into somebody else's in a

clear, spontaneous, memorable way—memorable for both you and your listeners.

Using your core-theme as a trampoline, you are going to break down your topic into three interlocking, forward-moving elements. All of these fit into what Miss Grumpy-puss would call the "body" of your talk. As you can see, her three-part form and the one we are dealing with here are apples and oranges.

Shaping a plan with a reasoned-out point is the irreducible secret of "spontaneous" or "improvised" speeches. If you want to be noteless, you cannot be planless. To free your eyes from a prepared text, you must fix your mind's eye on an outline that tames the topic while giving your thoughts a bright track to follow.

Blazing a trail you can remember—indeed "see" as an invisible path—requires you first to take two in-sequence steps. First, *break down the core-theme* (into two or more possible three-part plans); next, *let your conclusion choose the best plan.*

1. Breaking Down the Core-Theme

There's more than one way to skin a cat, and an endless array of possible breakdowns for almost any subject. The trick is to choose the best one—a plan of argument that can seduce the audience to your viewpoint.

In looking for the best plan, you should ask *three questions:* Which plan can best *simplify* your main facts and perspectives?; Which plan can best *illuminate* (as im-

ages) these facts and perspectives?; and Which plan can
best *advance* (i.e., pull forward) your line of argument?

Note that these questions together sum up a bedrock
rule about good speechmaking, and indeed good writing:
you should not try to overwhelm your audience with
words; instead, you should run a TV show, a movie documentary, before its eyes. You should put pictures, especially moving pictures, in peoples heads.

Why harp on visual impact?

First, because nearly everybody registers things he
sees more easily than things he *hears:* listen to a TV sitcom
for two minutes with your eyes closed, then watch it for
two minutes with the sound off, and you'll literally see.

Second, because in making a speech, as in writing an
article or a book, you are trying to capture and hold your
audience in the face of constant rivalry from boredom and
skepticism, if not hostility. It's tempting for an audience to
stop making the effort to follow a torrent of words, particularly if you talk in abstractions. If you are "showing" listeners an action-packed, colorful mental movie, they are
likely to hang in there (even if the movie is not obviously
Oscar-bound) and let your pretty pictures flow painlessly
into their consciousness.

This is not some shoot-from-the-lip theory I'm laying
on you. Scientists have hooked people up to brain-wave
machines and shown a big difference in the amount of at-
tention-effort a person puts into reading words on a page,
hearing a radio, or watching TV. Television takes by far
the least effort—the terms "idiot box" or "boob tube"
might apply to the medium even if the little screen ran Na-

tional Geographic specials every night instead of the Gong Show.

Are you tuned in now to paying as much care to your video track as to your "audio portion"? Let's look at some typical kinds of core-theme breakdowns.

Remember, for every subject many breakdowns are conceivable. We're going to skip through several breakdowns on a single theme to see—really "see"—which one would make the best TV show, the most gripping movie documentary.

This time imagine yourself as your country's ambassador to the United Nations. Far out? Maybe, but doing the Walter Mitty hour is probably helpful here to ease the lurch from one hypothetical plan to another.

You are seated at the Round Table of the Security Council at U.N. headquarters in New York. A crisis has flamed again in that key flashpoint of world geopolitics, Neurasthenia. The Neurotics (as modern diplomacy names the natives) have launched an unprovoked attack on their peace-loving neighbors in Dipsomania (land of the legendary Dipsos of archeological fame).

Your dilemma? The nasty Neurotics are allies of the freedom-folk of the West; the devastated Dipsos are allies of our all-fronts enemy, the Soviet Union.

Frankly, you don't know what the hell to say. You want to get your errant allies, the Neurotics, out of Dipsomania with as much elegance as possible—and without giving the Soviets a chance to play the saviors of civilization.

We'll assume you have already scanned your audience and brainstormed the topic as set out in the previous chapter. You have come up with a core-theme called "The Neurotic-Dipso Crisis: a Family Quarrel in Perspective."

The usefully vague term "perspective," of course, carries the exquisite hint that most people have got your allies' action all wrong. You, the sober-second-thought artist, will use this umbrella word and the homey "family" metaphor to downplay the whole episode.

We're going to run this fascinating theme through five different plans, then pick the one we think might fly. Remember, our goal is to explain the Neurotic invasion in an informative, tactful way that will press the invaders to withdraw quickly, with face-saving all around.

a) *Plan A: Chronological:* Splitting a theme into three convenient chunks of history is often the simplest and most convincing approach for political events. It forces you to rely on some version of the facts, and it carries the built-in dynamic of advancing time.

You begin by claiming that the only way to understand the invasion in depth is to set it in the telling context of history. The story of relations between Neurotics and Dipsos, indeed, takes on revealing nuances when you identify the three major phases of this movie, secretly entitled *Tale of the Warring Cousins:*

Part I: **The Medieval Phase:** *also known to specialists as the "family" phase. "During the Dark Ages, these now-hostile peoples were in fact one, a united tribe ruled over by a benign despot called Igor XVI. This common origin is vital to grasping the bitter, almost fratricidal, nature of later quarrels."*

Part II: **The Early Modern Phase:** *sometimes termed the* "rival-prince" *phase.* *"In the mid-nineteenth century, the Crown of the United Tribe fell victim to a brutal rivalry between the identical-twin sons of King Rathskeller III. The two princes, raised by separate tutors (one using the Latin alphabet, the other the Cyrillic) seized on differences in their education to insist that each had claim to half the Crown—each one reasoning that half a crown is better than none. Court jurists, eager to prevent civil war, proclaimed that two crowns did indeed exist, and this simple, peace-saving device led to the creation of the two states we know today, with their achingly interlocking interests."*

Part III: **The Contemporary Phase:** *known sometimes as the* "soul-sister" *phase.* *"Alas, the legal fiction of two crowns never did stir the hearts of these two stout branches of a single people. Ever since the split, their ancestral aspirations (backed by easily understandable economic solidarities) have been throwing them back into each other's arms. It is in the light of this somewhat pathetic yearning that we must view the saddening incursion of Neurotic troops into a territory they truly and deeply feel belongs to them.*

"My government, which stands for the sanctity of all existing borders and for self-determination of peoples, cannot condone this episode. But we must recall the noble sentiments of our friends the Neurotics. As a result, we ask this Council to limit its action to a mere reprimand of the Neurotic government, to a mediation mission to explore ways of reconciling the warring cousins, and to a possible program of aid to both peoples—

a program that eschews sterile sanctions in favor of the
U.N.'s deeper purposes of reconstruction and brother-
hood."

The whole plea, of course, reeks of shiftiness, and
serves up whoppers wrapped in euphemism. But we are,
after all, dealing in diplomacy. The point we're making
here is merely to show how a carefully carved-up period of
history can be mobilized to back the argument your government has ordered you to defend: that Neurotics are really just mixed-up kids.

Whenever you do get trapped into a chronological
plan, you can bring the time-frames alive for your audience
much better by sticking a pictorial label on each period.
For example, instead of droning on about the medieval,
early modern, and contemporary phases, you could highlight as titles (at the start, repeating them as you move
through the plan) the slightly jazzier ones of the "family,
rival-prince, and soul-sister" phases.

In this case, you would use the medieval, early modern, and contemporary terms as subtitles. Their descrip-
tiveness of the long evolution of the ages could give your
pitch a faint whiff of academic class and, of course, an air
of relentless progress.

Inexorability, indeed, is the key to a compelling plan.
The inner dynamic of your plan's structure should drag the
audience with you, your thoughts, your examples—and, in
the end, your conclusion.

b) *Plan B: Logical:* Let's try to stay inexorable, but
maybe get a whisker less fanciful. This time around, we'll

make our theme—the pardonable slip of our Neurotic friends—come alive, and move along, in a film your mind entitles (with apologies to Vittorio de Sica) *Bread, Love, and Revolution.* The idea here will be to show how economic conditions and cultural values pushed the half-vast Kingdom of Neurasthenia to commit the military version of incest. As we often claim to excuse sins of the flesh, one thing leads to another.

Part I: **The Economic Causes of War ("Bread"):** *"The root cause of the Neurotic border-crossing can be traced to economic inequality sharpened by cultural differences. When the Crown of the United Tribe split into two states in the mid-nineteenth century, most industry was installed on the Neurotic side, while vital food and raw materials stayed on the Dipso side. To exert political blackmail, the Dipsos raised prices, set quotas, and otherwise squeezed the Neurotic lifelines of prosperity, even survival."*

Part II: **The Cultural Causes ("Love"):** *"It would be ungallant to hint that our Neurotic friends crossed their new border merely for crass material gain. As a people deeply committed to divine guidance and preservation of ancestral values, they also felt obliged to protect more than three hundred twenty historic shrines (temples and museums, mainly) being desecrated by the rapacious farming methods of their Dipso cousins. Think of the Taj Mahal or St. Peter's Basilica being converted into pigpens, and you will grasp the spiritual indignation galvanizing the God-fearing folk of Neurasthenia."*

Part III: **The Inevitable Breakout ("Revolution"):**
*"Wounded in both stomach and heart, in both livelihood
and culture, could the people of Neurasthenia have
crossed their arms and allowed their very life-force to be
snuffed out? My government thinks not. And that is why
we plead for understanding, not condemnation. The
military reflex of our Neurotic friends was nothing more
than an act of legitimate self-defense. As such, it calls
for a solution which reaches beyond knee-jerk punish-
ment to reunite two peoples who, in more ways than
they or the legalists know, are really one (slightly
schizophrenic) nation."*

Dry your eyes, suspend disbelief again, and move on to

c) *Plan C: Escalating (or Concentric):* Here the
idea is to build a forward-driving tension into a very photo-
genic pattern of expanding circles: small to large, center to
outside edge. This can prove a good fit for an approach
using geography: local, regional, national; or, as we'll try
now, nation, continent, world. Call this mind's-eye movie
Distance Lends Enchantment:

Part I: **A Nation of Neurotics:** *"Seen as a purely
local, or national, event, the Neurotics' border-crossing
is doubtless a traumatic affair. For the two hundred
thirty-seven thousand inhabitants of this ebullient country, a war with neighboring Dipsomania stands as an
historic upset on the scale of the Crusades, if not the
Second World War. No one, certainly not my government, would wish to deny this."*

Part II: **A Continent in Transition:** *"Projected, however, against the seething background of the continent shared by the two antagonists with seventeen other nations, the dispute can be seen to fit a common pattern of cyclical frontier adjustments. At this very moment, nine other countries in the area are settling border claims by feats of arms. Plainly, in this part of the world, sending a couple of regiments through customs without passports is pretty well par for the course."*

Part III: **The World View: Much Ado About Nothing:** *"Expanding our outlook still further to embrace the whole globe, we can see that the Neurotic-Dipso matter pales into triviality. With China and Russia squaring off, and the H-bomb proliferating into San Marino and Lichtenstein, frankly, my friends, the U.N. has bigger fish to fry. Boys will be boys, Neurotics will be neurotics, and Dipsos will be dipsomaniacs. In short, let's forget the whole silly comic-opera caper."*

Unthinkable, this ploy? Insulting to the diplomatic intelligence? Remember the Japanese government's doublespeak when its army occupied all of Chinese Manchuria in 1931–32? Tokyo's lads in striped pants, taking a world view, termed this exercise "the Manchurian *incident*." When the Soviets sent Warsaw Pact divisions to subjugate Alexander Dubček's Czechoslovakia in 1968, they called it "normalization" required by "international socialist solidarity."

When you want to downplay something in a three-part plan, sink it in an ever-widening context.

For our next number, let's get

d) *Plan D: Analytical:* This time, we're going to be-
fuddle our Security Council colleagues by taking the topic
apart as a policy process: people, leaders, goals. Here the
dynamic pushing plan, speaker, and audience along in-
volves tracing how the aspirations and fears of a nation
flow from voters to elected leaders into state objectives.

How? Inevitably, we hope to show—in a mind's-eye
movie we'll call *The March to Democratic War:*

> *Part I:* **The People (Source of Policy):** *"Even in
> totalitarian states, the goals of government must mirror
> a broad consensus of citizens. In a democracy such as
> Neurasthenia, people can lay down directions both ac-
> tively and specifically. The fact is, native Neurotics want
> to reunite the many families split by the century-old state
> schism, and reap the benefits of welding together again
> the two complementary economies. At the last elections,
> Neurotic voters put in power a government mandated to
> seek new negotiations with Dipsomania to this end."*

> *Part II:* **The Leaders (Shapers of Policy):** *"The Gov-
> ernment of Neurasthenia is a peace-loving and patient
> regime, but it was instructed by a democratic vote to
> take all steps needed to bring the two countries into a
> new relationship. This did not mean Anschluss or forced
> union, merely a cooperative link allowing a humane so-
> lution to the split-family problem and harmonizing the
> two matching economies. Dipsomania refused all nego-
> tiation on these points, thus frustrating a democratic
> people in its legitimate hopes."*

Part III: **Goals (the Evolution of Policy):** *"The Government of Neurasthenia, blocked in its reasonable diplomatic quest, had to assess all available means to pursue its people's hopes. Words failing, and an economic boycott proving ineffective, the Government was pressed to restate these goals in military terms. In this light, the border-crossing must be seen merely as a crowbar to pry open serious negotiations with a regime hostile to civilized talks. The armed action is not an invasion; it is a tragically necessary last resort to achieve a people's fairminded goals."*

Shades of Danzig, of course, or of almost any war of aggression you care to think of. But catch the tortured reasoning, feel self-righteously indignant, and tell yourself how neatly you could pull such a plan on a local lumber company resisting your sweet-talking takeover bid.

Now a quickie, using Hegel's Ping-Pong tension: the dialectic.

e) *Plan E: Dialectical:* The idea here, you'll recall, is to create a "what next?" feeling between the three parts by moving from black to white to gray: thesis-antithesis-synthesis. Your secret movie-title could be *The Best of Both Worlds.*

Part I: **The Unitary Straitjacket:** *"History proved that corralling Neurotics and Dipsos into one country could not work. Local differences in economic resources and religious beliefs gave the Crown of the United Tribes what Lord Durham said in 1839 of English and French*

Canadians: 'two nations warring in the bosom of a single state.'"

Part II: **The Unstable Rivals:** *"On the other hand, later history (that since the Crown split) showed that the 'separated brethren,' the Neurotics and the Dipsos, could neither survive economically nor coexist politically without war-inducing tension."*

Part III: **The Confederation Compromise:** *"Since neither extreme (one centralized state or two independent states) can work, can anyone doubt that peace and prosperity lie somewhere in between? The answer, combining autonomy with solidarity, is a true confederation —a loose pooling of sovereignties in an umbrella-state holding powers of defense, foreign affairs, and broad economic coordination, with each participating state (Neurasthenia and Dipsomania) free,* in extremis, *to secede. Paradoxically, it is this very granting of the right of secession which, by buttressing a sense of secure particularism, will guarantee that neither state ever bothers to secede.*

"In placing the Neurotic incursion within this framework of options, my government prefers to seize the immediate military event as an opportunity to encourage both sides to negotiate this long-overdue coming to terms with common sense."

Don't blame me. Diplomats talk that way all the time.

Just notice, as you raise your hand to vote, that this plan, the dialectical one, also happens to be a textbook "chronological" or "historical" plan. Two plans, each with its own internal movement, each reinforcing the other. Planwise, a double plan is very wise. Dynamite.

Now relax. Let your mind unwind from these procedural games.

Before we pick the best plan of the five we tried, don't forget that you or I easily could embroider a dozen other half-decent plans to explain this diplomatic Disneyland, and still get our Neurotic allies out more or less intact. Just offhand, I would recommend you have a go at several allegorical plans—plans using the imagery and even jargon of, say, medicine, plumbing, accounting, aviation, farming, and investment. These are plans you can lay on a specific professional audience (of doctors, plumbers, etc.). For clarity and warmth, you should also imagine a three-part plan for children, using fairy-tale analogies: who's afraid of the big bad wolf? The Dipsos, that's who. And so on.

In sum, the whole lengthy example of you as a U.N. ambassador served as a teaching tool. It was a game to illustrate the unlimited variety of three-part plans you can cook up to convince your audience that your conclusion is right—because your argumentation seems irresistible.

As we turn now to letting the most convincing conclusion lead us back to the punchiest plan, remember that plan-picking should partly rely on whom you're talking to.

A good plan needs as much as possible to be "tailor made" to your audience. Philosophers groove on history. Military people might like a geographic plan (situation, topography, geopolitics, with a tip of the hat to Montesquieu's theory relating landscape and climate to political beliefs).

Everybody loves a plan based on three issue-incarnating personalities. An old newspaper trick: work in lots of names. They add life and constructive voyeurism.

To rev yourself up for this fascinating game of plan-playing, by the way, drench yourself sometime in the virtuoso variations of Cyrano de Bergerac in his "tirade of the nose." If he can dredge up that many ways of mocking his own nose, you can hatch at least as many hilarious (and often plausible) plans for three-part seductions of your listeners.

2. Letting Your Conclusion Choose the Plan

What a genius you are. You have devised at least five plans for the same topic. Your only problem now: *l'embarras du choix*, an embarrassment of riches. How do you grab the right ball and run?

First, go back to the three questions we asked at the start of this chapter on breaking down the core-theme. Your benchmarks for a sound plan are: simplicity, illumination, and advancement (dynamics).

Keep these in mind as you look back over the various possible plans you thought up. Remember, though, that the *clincher* in choosing the best plan has to be the *conclusion* ("Part III") which these benchmarks led you to.

The decisive question now is: which conclusion (based on its underpinning arguments in the first two parts) is most likely to come alive for the special audience at hand? If you intend to give roughly the same spiel to several different audiences—audiences of distinctive age, cultural or professional characteristics—which conclusion seems powerful and vivid enough to rope in almost any fair-minded person?

If your audience is known to be hostile to your thinking, you might even replay your arguments in a "shoe on the other foot" or "science fiction" approach. This tack can work well when you are facing an audience with long-fixed or merely prejudiced views.

Take the U. S. Civil War. The simple device of asking Northerners to imagine how they would feel now about a whole series of people and policies *if the South had won* can shake your listeners loose from set opinions more quickly than months of learned lectures. The same goes for Canadians. If you're an English-speaking Canadian, imagine that the French had won the Battle of the Plains of Abraham in 1759 and that your province—Ontario, say, or Saskatchewan—remained the only English enclave in an overwhelmingly French North America. How long would it take you to want a law making English the only official language in your province? How long to form a separatist party? How long to want to fly airplanes in English in your home province even though the "majority" people told you "French is the international language of aviation"?

This little trick can work with almost any three-part plan—but use it sparingly and with wit. Most people can swallow a hard message about their own prejudice only if you leave them a face-saving exit. Humor, and especially hyperbole, offers a precious escape hatch to healthier attitudes.

Now let's look at some examples of plan-picking. As one last whack at the Neurotic-Dipso saga, I would confirm Plan E ("dialectical") as my first all-purpose choice. Dialectical plans in general carry more forward-moving tension (the "inexorability" factor) than perhaps any other kind. And here we were able to beef up the plan, to spur its dynamic flow, by making it coincide with a bona fide chronological plan. Moreover, this plan offers good "telegenic" possibilities: two rivals in one straitjacket must choose compromise or agony. For specialized audiences, all you need to "put pictures in people's heads" would be to graft onto the heading of each part, and perhaps of main subheadings (we'll come to that soon), concrete, colorful images on, say, house-building or a juicy love affair.

Injecting A Telegenic Allegory

(Neurotic-Dipso caper)

House-building en Famille:

- *The Single-Family Dwelling* (one unitary state): crowded, thus contentious
- *Two Houses Apart* (two separate states): too costly to build and to keep up
- *A Condominium Duplex* (the confederation compromise): room for both peoples under a single roof at reasonable cost

Or, taking the romantic route:

Living with Your Lover:

- *The Double-Bed Dispute* (one unitary state): Not even a water bed could accommodate two lovers who disagreed on nocturnal cracker-nibbling.

- *The Crosstown Apartment Split* (two separate states): Apartments mean apart, and parting is such suite sorrow as, both emotionally and economically, the lovers find that out of sight is not out of sight at all—just out of mind.
- *Twin-Bed Harmony* (the confederation compromise): Sharing a room, but not a bed, solves the cracker crisis and saves both rent and relationship.

I wouldn't try that one at the U.N., but I certainly would at the Elks' Club ladies' auxiliary. Tasteful, unsmirking, subliminal sex has been known to pay amazing dividends. A chapter on groupies will appear in my next book.

Branching away from Walter Mitty on the East River, let's nail down our plan-picking technique with a couple of closer-to-grassroots examples. Let's say you're a union leader in California's Napa Valley and you're fighting for a better deal for grape pickers. You are facing an influential but unsympathetic audience of bankers with a lot of money behind the growers.

Your first challenge is to *cut to a core-theme* that will most likely send a charge of adrenaline through your listeners. You decide to pour out a gallon or two of the red ink the bankers fear may run if too many growers go belly up because of high wages, thus defaulting on their loans. Save the appeals to charity and human solidarity until you have zapped their pin-striped minds with a chilling vision of bankruptcy. The ploy must be, as in any plea to an adversary, to dig out and display the audience's self-interest —though in a way that reveals how its interests can mesh with yours.

Next you must *sketch out four or five likely plans: historical* (risky, because it inevitably drags out all kinds of off-putting past injustices and angers); *dialectical* (strong on advocacy, but tending to rub noses in arguments rooted in antagonism); *geographic* (narrow, thus weak, not a gut-grabber); *personality-based* (vivid and riveting if well painted, but you could trivialize the whole debate as a mere conflict between badly matched individuals); *analytical* (this one, if you kept closely to the audience's own self-interest as the core-theme, could well be a winner.)

Why would the analytical plan probably prove the most persuasive? Because if you *imagine the conclusion* you intend to reach (better wages for grape pickers will strengthen the grape and wine industry by ending costly fighting and by raising productivity with more eager workers), you can backtrack through an argumentation in Parts I and II that naturally establishes mind-opening solidarities.

Example:

Mixing Movement And Allegory

(The Body-Builders:
Growers, Bankers, and Workers)

Part I: **The Growers** (*the bone structure*): *More than owners, they are managers with the incentive of ownership. Their lifetime professional commitment offers the industry stability, strength, structure.*

Part II: **The Bankers** (*the lifeblood*): *By pumping money into the vineyard system created by the growers, bankers bring life, growth, and hope.*

Part III: **The Workers** (*the muscle and heart*): *In a sensibly ordered industry, workers should be encouraged to contribute not just brawn, but enthusiasm. To give this, they must be treated with dignity, both moral and material. They must be treated not as peons but as partners: with decent pay, social benefits, and a secure job. These are the union's goals. They are also the key to any long-term growth, a dramatic rise in productivity, and thus the shared prosperity of growers, bankers, and workers.*

No doubt you would need a little more than that to reconcile all of California's growers and workers. But the aim here is to illustrate a *rhetorical strategy.* You are trying to use a plan structure to underline a natural alliance between antagonists presumed irreconcilable.

Surprise, symmetry, a credible allegory with colorful imagery, momentum leading up to a spotlight on the group you want to draw sympathy for—all this you get from this simple analytical plan.

Why? Because you let your conclusion—the overlooked solidarity of old enemies—dictate a step-by-step argumentation able to unplug hostile ears. First you decided to stress the adversaries' complementary roles in making everybody prosper. From there, the backtrack through the separate roles (in more or less the order followed) was almost irresistible.

This sense of inevitability must mark every gripping conclusion. Your listeners must come almost to mutter to themselves, "Ah, of course. *Now* I see." You must click on a light in their minds. You must make them Sauls on the road to Damascus, fellow-travelers to *your* home base, surprised but delighted converts. You must sweep them along with you, make them feel they are your copilots on a flight to an unsuspected truth.

Try one last shot at letting an "inevitable" conclusion dictate your choice of plan. This time you are a welfare mother who has decided to get off the dole and start up a one-woman secretarial agency at home. Why not? You're young, healthy, and smart. Your listeners at a YWCA seminar are sympathetic but skeptical.

Offhand, I'd say the two main factors you ought to look for in a core-theme here are motivation and practicality. They are, of course, linked; and in cooking up a conclusion we should try to work them both in. It seems to me our general idea for both core-theme and conclusion ought to be something like *workable dignity*. One likes to presume that any audience, except perhaps one of wounded welfarecrats, would find this aspiration laudable.

We'll have a go at *four alternative plans*. Here we'll start with values or other dynamic factors as our building blocks, then extrapolate the plan's structure (analytical, etc.) from these. As factors, we'll use psychology, technology, finances, and sexual politics. No doubt all those and more would enter into a real decision to swap dependency for independence, (welfare) checks for (bank) balances.

As a welfare mom, you would likely decide to leave the drugging embrace of the social workers because of some deep-felt psychological need—a taste for self-reliance, or at least a distaste for licking boots and food stamps.

Your *psychological plan* should therefore lead listeners to share this taste, by stressing the delights of going-it-alone freedom. A fair three-part plan might first state self-respect as your ultimate goal; then note how welfare destroys this; then bounce to an accounting of the spiritual, as well as practical, superiority of running your own show. The last part could spell out some down-to-earth ways you could attain and savor your independent joys.

This plan, you can see, has elements of both the deductive (stating the principle or goal, then seeking ways to reach it) and the dialectical (a nicely wrenching Ping-Pong between welfare and enterprise as options). The two structures launch you on a rather thrilling little crescendo toward your conclusion that getting out of the public trough makes you feel better—and probably gives the five-year-old daughter you dote on a readier chance to flower too.

A *technology-based plan* could be fun as an exercise in exploring new physical opportunities. It could start by noting that until about 1980 welfare mothers were kept from office, store, or factory work because they had to stay home to care for their children. Then it could announce that microprocessors with telephone links called Modems could now allow an astute woman to work "in" an outside office by working at home and sending her paperwork in by telephone. Finally, this plan could project ahead ten years to list three or four more technological break-throughs (videotex, cheaper telecopiers, and TV tele-phones) which might virtually wipe out the home-vs.-office dilemma for welfare mothers—at least for those, like you, harboring small children but large brains and self-esteem.

Such a plan, obviously, is basically chronological. But it offers the added momentum of accelerating technological progress—a strong sweep forward to your conclusion about a new era when all we'll have to worry about is welfare fathers.

A *money-based plan* could start with a depressing reminder of how the lack of a cash-providing husband and the option of working outside the home traps welfare mothers in near-permanent bankruptcy. Then it could show how this dead end is perpetuated by outdated credit policies which refuse to glimpse the human potential in many welfare mothers. Finally, the plan could lead from this failing of imagination to a package of farsighted new loan policies designed to *invest* in such trapped women instead of *subsidizing* them: long-term, government-backed "soft" loans, courses in running a business from home (possibly even a franchised day-care center), free bookkeeping, and plenty of free advice.

This plan rests on a momentum of hope. It moves strongly from despair to optimism by gradually guiding us to unthought-of but simple and practical opportunities. All because some sensible politician—that rarest of reformers —thought of putting ideas before money, and thus made money serve ideas.

You could term this a logical (effect-cause-solution) or analytical plan, with a dash of the chronological to buttress it.

Last but not lubriciously at all, let's ponder a *sexual-politics plan*. These days, when the world is no longer as safe as it was for endearing cads, blaming the whole mess of welfare mothers on men is a tempting orthodoxy. Men goof off, and their female victims sound off—often for good cause, but the men are still stupid enough to forget that in any argument the absent are always wrong.

Your plan here takes as core-theme and conclusion the idea that we must move from phallocracy to democracy. Your goal is to persuade wandering males that, after flying the coop, they can come home to roost without either needing to rule it or feeling henpecked. As with the bankers and the grape pickers, you want to seduce wayward daddies into seeing an undreamed-of coincidence of interests between themselves and their abandoned women and children.

Your three-part plan could start by reviewing the evidence of the New Biology (which is the oldest of all) that males of most species really do need to stray, because they are programmed by nature to enrich the species as widely as possible. Then having bashed the boys a bit, you could recall how women (through biological or cultural factors?) worsen matters with their "Cinderella complex," as the best-selling book of that title showed—their tendency, even when ostensibly stand-alone stalwarts, to lie in ambush for a Prince Charming with bags of gold to take them to life's Palace Ball. Finally, you could conclude that male paranoia and the female nesting instinct should still allow intelligent modern couples to work out an original synthesis to stay in each other's territorial waters—some tailor-made equivalent of mooring two sailboats a hundred yards apart, with mommy and the kid in one boat, and a "free" but available daddy nearby to share fish and winds.

Forgive me—we're waxing unintentionally poetic. But since we did, why not backtrack to graft our boating anal-

ogy onto the whole plan? Part one could have the man
seizing unilateral power by sailing aimlessly after exotic
fish and winds all over the ocean; part two could portray
the woman as plotting power traps by lying in wait near
shore with her net to catch passing fishermen; and part
three could show the new democratic synthesis of shared
responsibility for water-space and children.

In short, this approach portrays a crude and uncon-
ventional, but maybe psychologically workable, form of
democracy. It is a hybrid of analytical and dialectical
plans.

Naturally (I hear the protests already), only a male
chauvinist pig would think up such an absurd and pa-
tronizing arrangement. Please don't judge. Don't even try
living this way. Just try to flow with the plan-playing tide.

Which of these conclusions strikes you as the
strongest? Personally, I think our first plan, the psychological one, most satisfyingly fits our three standards: simplicity (the easy-to-grasp premise of wanting dignity); illumination (we focus on people, not abstractions such as
interest rates); and advancement (the deductive and partly
dialectical tensions move us along forcefully).

However, I prefer the psychological plan mostly because I think that, more than the others, it gets to the bottom of things: it emphasizes a thirst for self-reliance and
dignity as the welfare mother's key motivation. I like the
nitty-gritty realism of the technology-based and money-
based plans, but for a topic with such deep human
significance, I would only use such angles as possible sub-

sections of a main plan which digs into issues of the heart and spirit.

Our final plan, the sexual-politics one, does a bit of that as well. But its bias is narrowly biological.

Besides, in that last one, I think that as we sail into the sunset we get shipwrecked on the shoals of a less-than-credible allegory. We might do better with the chicken-coop imagery. Yet even there we risk, so to speak, laying an egg. Roosters and hens are a bit too jokey for a plight that few find funny.

The three conclusions we rejected—new technology creates new opportunities, more imaginative financing can help, and separate-but-nearby residences might work—are all "plumbing" solutions. They offer mere technical or mechanical devices for getting the women and their children off the dole. These approaches could be fine for an audience of scientists, bankers, or sailors. But for a broader audience, one with a cross section of human perspectives, I think our conclusion about finding dignity for the woman and her daughter is more compelling. So, if you set your sights high, I would argue that this conclusion is unavoidable.

In all three of our examples—the Neurotic-Dipso saga, the bankers–grape pickers pitch, and the welfare-mother adventure, this sense of our conclusion's inevitability led us to our "ideal" plan. You may well query my choices of conclusions, and therefore of plans; perhaps your values and tastes differ from mine. No matter. You have reasoned through the *process* of choosing among alternatives, and that is all we wanted to do.

Is plan-shaping starting to feel unavoidable? I hope so. But mastering the knack of winging it is still not quite unavoidable. To get really close to takeoff in our Tiger Moth, we must now toss some canvas on our fuselage.

Histories make men wise; poets witty; the mathematics, subtle; natural philosophy, deep; morals, grave; logic and rhetoric, able to contend.

—SIR FRANCIS BACON

CHAPTER FIVE

Fleshing Out Your Plan

So here you are with a brilliant, persuasive three-part line of argument. This outline will remain as your teleprompter (or mind's-eye script) throughout your speech. But an audience, like a lover, wants to embrace more than a skeleton. It needs to feel the flesh, the contours, the delightful detail of the "body" of your talk. Rounding off your speech requires two steps: filling in your three-part structure, then wrapping up the introduction and ending.

1. Filling In Your Three-Part Structure

Unless you're stuck with a real caught-with-your-pants-down stump speech, or given less than five minutes

to talk, you should work out ahead of time a well-fitting, il-
lustrative mini-plan for each of your three main sections.
This is where you find out whether you really do know the
subject, whether your research or background is deep
enough to let you paint a fresco over a cartoon.

As with the big three-part picture, your mini-plans for
subsections should respect the Bauhaus rule of architecture: form follows function. *For subsections,* however,
already anchored in the framework of the overall plan, you
need not repeat our by-now obsessive three-part outline.
Two to five (no more) parts will be fine, for you can structure each subsection any way you want—as long as it
works.

Making the subsections "work" means making them
reinforce your whole speech's point. It means strengthening
the general three-part plan. It means satisfying your audience's curiosity about what's in the nooks and crannies of
your argument.

The guideposts for breaking down each of the three
main parts into subsections are the same as for the main
parts themselves:

- **Simplify:** to their bare bones the arguments supporting your core-theme

- **Illuminate:** these arguments aptly and vividly
  (with concrete examples)

- **Advance:** the argumentation relentlessly by placing the subsections in a naturally dynamic order;
  i.e., each subsection must whet the listener's appetite to hear what's next

Remember, you are running a movie—a *moving picture*—before your audience. Your overall plan has laid
down the three main acts, the way the theme unfolds, and
the denouement. Your subsections must add the finer
points of pacing, characterization, mood, and, above all,
confirming highlights:

a) *The "Picture" Element:* The absolutely vital job
you've got to pull off now is dreaming up the precise images that mean something to the audience at hand. As
Chapter Nine will show, examples, anecdotes, even jokes
should fit your listeners' frame of reference—cultural, edu-
cational, professional, economic, whatever.

b) *The "Moving" Element:* As you try to simplify, illuminate, and advance, it doesn't matter whether your "mini-
plan" for each subsection rests on a logical, chronological,
analytical, allegorical, or any other basis. But the basis
must be *systematic* and *forward-moving*. That's what we're
after. Now let's look at a three-part skeleton with some
subsection flesh on it.

In your latest incarnation you are a woman (or conceivably a far-sighted man) giving a forty-minute talk to
sell the Equal Rights Amendment or just plain old
Women's Lib. Your audience? A bunch of crusty old gents
from your friendly local legislature. To sway these guys,
your whole plan—the three-part overall outline and your
subsection mini-plans—will, of course, be simple and colorful, and carry megatons of movement. It will enrich these
virtues with gobs of "audience-apt" color, and as much
unthreatening humor as your seething soul can allow.

To make it easier to focus on our subsections, we'll make our main outline a simple chronological one. By using history as raw material, you will keep your talk factual (and thereby open to ready illustration), and it will have a natural forward movement.

After we've seen how this plan underpins the subsections that we'll work out, we'll show you how the same subsections could work just as well with three other plans. Let's glance first at our chronological plan:

EQUALITY FOR WOMEN—WHO GAINS MOST?

Detailed Subsection Breakdown

(Within a Chronological Main Outline)

Our main outline slides you ahead from one era to another as follows:

    I. Early View of Women's Lib
    II. Current View of Women's Lib
    III. The Future Shaped by Women's Lib
    Let's take each part in turn:

Part I: EARLY VIEW OF WOMEN'S LIB

Remember again: you do *not* need to split all your subsections into three parts. That would trap you into a too-rigid format, a kind of singsong ritual that could end up with you sounding like a parrot declaiming kindergarten math. It's rare that you would ever go farther than four or five subsections; once you do, you tend to get lost. Besides, using two to four parts varies your rhythm of argument and is quite enough to make you sound both interesting and spontaneous.

In this first part, we'll split the "Early View of Women's Lib" into two main subsections. The first one ("Root Injustices") splits further into four sub-subsections, the second ("Flowering Inferno") into three sub-subsections.

Note that the dynamic moving you from "Root Injustices" to "Flowering Inferno" rests on cause and effect. We look first at underlying biological, cultural, social, and economic factors; then we see how these led to women achieving "reform" by writing, demonstrating, and karate-chopping. Note also that each sub-subsection carries its own forward-moving force: biology (the life-force) leads to culture (as an instinctive way of life) to society (as an organized way of life for personal relationships) to economics (an organized way of life refined to embrace exchanges of goods and services). You get the same forward movement in the three sub-subsections of "Flowering Inferno": feminist writers agitate demonstrators, some of whom move from street marches to frightening nice young men with kung fu.

Have a look at the following to see what we're talking about. Take your time. This is simpler than it seems. Just slow down and ponder each step in our progress. To keep on track, you may find it helpful to check back to the paragraph preceding this one as you read through the breakdown.

Here's our subsection breakdown for Part I then: "Early View of Women's Lib." To catch the forward momentum, imagine that the "roots" of subsection A grow into the "flowers" of subsection B:

Part I: EARLY VIEW OF WOMEN'S LIB

A. **Root Injustices** (our breakdown of this sub-subsection is analytical, also cause-effect):

1. *Biological:* physiological "drawbacks" (women have less strength, but more pregnancy, than men) lay the basis for inequality.

2. *Cultural:* women are put down in religion, in literature, and now even in popular culture (detergent-ad ding-a-lings).

3. *Social:* male bonding, dress, and the concept of "lady" inhibit men's psychological acceptance of women's equality (it's hard to look a statue on a pedestal in the eye).

4. *Economic:* job discrimination: women enjoy less access to jobs and get paid less. As the economy gradually needs more women, this becomes the toughest pressure point (male Ph.D.'s may at least drive taxis; female ones must settle for go-fer jobs).

B. **Flowering Inferno:** This shows how the above root injustices led to spontaneous combustion (our next sub-subsection breakdown uses escalation to move the topic from ideas to progressively more violent action:

1. *Authors:* Betty Friedan, Germaine Greer, Kate Millett (these pioneers planted the seeds of sedition in a male-run world).

2. *Demonstrators:* burning bras was burning bridges.

3. *Karate choppers:* Ti-Grace Atkinson: chops that hinted at castration?

Are you getting the idea? We are moving your argument—and listeners—along in short, self-advancing sequences of logic. These fit neatly into your overall three-part plan, but they vary its pace and create interesting little internal tensions which drive you on cheerfully to your conclusion. Having set the stage with the early days of women's awakening, let's see next how we can satisfy our listeners' now-whetted curiosity by breaking down the second of our three parts:

Part II: CURRENT VIEW OF WOMEN'S LIB
This time we shall again use two subsections to contain, illustrate, and move along our nitty-gritty sub-subsections. Our subsection A ("Economic Colonialism") aims to sketch out a bad situation, a man-over-woman domination which, instinctively in subsection B ("Economic Decolonization"), we will want to correct: a set-up case of showing listeners an evil, then removing it. If you need to get academic about this breakdown, tell yourself you are riding a dynamic of evolutionary contrast—the rise and fall of males' power over money. Doesn't that thought make you angry, ecstatic, or something?

Look ahead now to the sub-subsections of A and B. We have for you here a symmetrical little surprise, a gimmick you always wanted for Christmas: two successive pairs of sub-subsections bouncing ahead on a dynamic of economic determinism.

"What, pray tell, is that?" I hear from the back rows. Just another tricky argument of your old pal and mine, Karl Marx, purporting to prove that whatever you think or do comes from the size of your wallet. More precisely, economic determinism argues that whoever controls the "means of production" (capital, plants, equipment, labor) decides how society will run—including customs, religion, music, love, and poker games.

The delight of this plausible if often fallacious reasoning is that it ties in perfectly with the larger A-B subsection-breakdown of colonialism and decolonization. It seems, at least, to sustain our forward momentum: correcting the abuse of male supremacy. In the first pair of sub-subsections (beginning "Men Control"), watch how we start by highlighting man's stranglehold over the economy to lead into his broader power in society. Then, in the second pair (beginning "Bedroom to Boardroom"), watch how we give women a trampoline of shared economic power to leap into power in many other, non-economic, fields.

Part II: CURRENT VIEW OF WOMEN'S LIB

A. Economic Colonialism:

1. *Men Control:* capital, management, unions (our economy is one great big Ku Klux Klan with no ladies' auxiliary).

2. *Men thus dominate:* politics, administration, culture (he who pays the piper calls the tunes).

B. Economic Decolonization:

1. *Bedroom to Boardroom:* In the past fifteen years women have captured professional outposts, then citadels: women's consumer power, added to infiltration of "male" careers, marks a female coup d'état ("L'état, c'est moi . . . et toi").

2. *"Home" Is Now Everywhere:* And so, at least in theory, is woman's place. ERA (political rights), Margaret Thatcher (political power), Jill Clayburgh (lifestyle freedom), and Edith Bunker (domestic dignity) all spell out a new power-sharing. Women-driver jokes are out; odd couples and henpecked husbands in.

Wasn't that fun? This whole business of injecting fresh momentum into your subsections and sub-subsections is a racy affair. Don't run out of breath, but use forward-moving logic even in these humbler corners of your speech to carry your listeners along. If you transport them with a bit. of order and grace, they'll never fall asleep.

Let's end off our filling-out game by working out a rhythm of argument for Part III which makes a pleasing conclusion. I find that in your final main part—which is usually this third one—you are better off avoiding too-fancy displays of sub-subsections. If you split, then resplit this wrap-up phase too much, you risk bogging down in detail. The detail should already have come in the first two main parts. Here, as we swoop toward a convincing ending, you should speed the pace noticeably by simplifying your structure. Accordingly, here we'll stick to a three-subsection breakdown of Part III, with no cluttering sub-subsections to slow us down.

The following A, B, C breakdown of Part III follows a kind of center-seeking or de-escalating dynamic. Without the frill of sub-subsections, this accelerates toward our conclusion, drawing us ever closer to the lusty heart of the matter.

Lusty? I knew that would get you to read on. But it's true. For our conclusion finds that equality, balance, and harmony mean a richer world for both sexes—especially for men, in these three public, family, and intimate areas:

Part III: THE FUTURE SHAPED BY WOMEN'S LIB

A. **In the workplace:** The macho compulsion to compete will be shared, thus diminished, by women's joining the rat race. Women may snag lots of top jobs, but also the ulcers and heart attacks that go with them. Freed from the tension of professional mating dances, men may live longer and find more satisfaction than confrontation at work. Moral: in losing the key to the executive washroom, man may find his soul.

B. **In the home:** Wearing the pants at home is not the ultimate issue. Deciding not to take out the garbage or fix light sockets may be. In a home where traditional roles fade, men can reconquer many areas properly theirs: cooking, sewing, and ironing are arts challenging to man's peculiar genius.

C. **In the boudoir:** Sooner or later, women's lib leads every man to ponder how the new equality will affect his joy on the conjugal battlefield. Surprise: this is precisely where he gains most. We can promise him not a rose garden, but a secret garden of fantasy: the woman liberated from economic and social oppression is a female freed from hangups, rage, resentment, and tactical headaches.

Never mind whether this whole line of argument strikes you as a fantasy. Again we are outlining a rhetorical strategy. This time we have spelled out the game plan from divisional level to brigade, regimental, and even platoon level.

Were all these subsections and sub-subsections a mere fluke, tied to the simplicity of a three-part chronological outline? Not at all. They could work equally well within a number of other types of main outline—not necessarily all (because imagery and even logic might not match), but within many types.

As evidence, just skip through these three other possible three-part main outlines which you could have used. Each one, you will see, uses a different dynamic to move listeners forward: each starts from a distinct bias. But as rhetorical rhythms, they interlock splendidly. And they allow you to improvise your subsection and sub-subsection structure to fit any and all of them.

EQUALITY FOR WOMEN—WHO GAINS MOST?

Alternative Three-Part Main Outlines

A. Chronological Plan (this, of course, is the one we just ran through):

    I. Early View of Women's Lib
    II. Current View of Women's Lib
    III. The Future Shaped by Women's Lib

B. Dialectical Plan:

    I. Woman's Gain (thesis)
    II. Man's Loss (antithesis)
    III. Both Sides Now (synthesis)

C. Evolutive Plan:

    I. Goal as Vengeance
    II. Goal as Power
    III. Goal as Balance

D. Escalating Plan:

    I. Mood of Anger
    II. Mood of Cool Determination
    III. Mood of Harmony

Now, that was not as hard as it looked, was it? Try inserting into the alternative plans all those subsection and sub-subsection breakdowns we did with the chronological plan. You'll see that they work well there too. Then, armed with all this practice and just enough theory to feed you without choking, you should be able to splinter your own speeches into a thousand—well, say a dozen—meaningful pieces.

Going back to the movie idiom, you now know how to write more than a treatment or a synopsis; you can dash off a subtly fleshed-out shooting script. With this, doing your speech amounts merely to turning on lights, camera, and action.

2. Wrapping Up the Introduction and Ending

But before we roll the film, a final matter of form, the icing on the cake. The icing—your introduction and ending—should please in relation to your plan the way icing tastes in relation to a cake: even better.

a.) *Why a Special Start and Finish:* In any speech or talk lasting over five minutes, your introduction and ending require almost as much care as the plan itself. I can think of plenty of basically bad speeches that were salvaged by a zingy introduction and ending. That does not mean you should rely on fireworks at the start and end to camouflage a crummy plan. You must simply give these two bookends of your talk your best shot: the introduction to grab your audience, your ending to leave an enduring impression.

Both start and finish must fit our concept of a speech as a moving picture. So try to make them do two jobs for your plan:

    (i) *Highlight the theme* (the "picture" element): In
a simple, deliberate statement, reduce the theme
(and each of its main parts) to an image or an
easy-to-grasp slogan.

   (ii) *Smooth the plan's flow* (the "moving" element):
Make a light, elegant reference to how the plan—
that is, the core-theme analyzed—moves.

Let's take the start and finish for a moment and sum
up their special goals. Note that neither start nor finish
should take up more than 5 percent of your speaking
time. If they do, you'll screw up the balance, even the
structure of your plan.

    b.) *What an Introduction and Ending Should Do:*
Even though both serve to highlight the theme and underline the plan's movement, each of these two tacked-on parts
of your speech fulfills these goals in its own way.

A short and attention-getting introduction does not
allow rambling anecdotes, elaborate jokes, or foggy allegories that back you cutely into your topic. Use imagery
that is apt and arresting, but above all—*get to the point.*

The "point"—the irreducible, down-to-earth job an
intro should do—includes three tasks: define the topic;
state your plan (just the three main parts); and telegraph
your conclusion.

Let's start with the start. Ideally, your introduction
should define your topic in one clear, strong sentence. If
you are assigned a formal title that is not very jazzy, use it.

Then immediately restate it in layman's language in one more sentence, if possible a vivid and concrete one.

An example for stock marketeers:

"Tonight I'm going to talk about investing in foreign currency futures—or betting on dreams with other people's money."

Presumably listeners crazy enough to dabble in currency futures came to hear precisely that topic. Here you have hit them bang off with what they want, but lightened the tone to let them know you are not merely going to drone on in gnomes-of-Zurich jargon.

Let's imagine next a briefing that you, as an Air Force colonel, are giving fighter pilots on a new fire-control system for air-to-air rockets:

"Gentlemen, today you're going to learn about our new hair-trigger-sensitive rocket-firing technology. Think of this challenge as the electronic equivalent of premature ejaculation."

That's a problem known to many young pilots, no doubt. You have their attention, and they have a very personal feel for the dangers of the untried hardware.

Now you are an art merchant, fresh back from the Yucatán with a tale of woe about archeological thievery:

"Stones, statues, and stealing. That's the story I'm going to tell you about how greedy philistines are destroying three thousand years of Mexican history."

They are indeed. And you've nailed your audience instantly with a razor-sharp topic and a 102-degree Fahrenheit reading of your anger.

Finally, cast yourself as president of Wilder Widgets,

Inc., as you launch the world's very first electric nit-picker for home use:

"Can Wilder Widgets leave any nit unpicked? We think not. And that's why you, our sales staff, will get the same 110 volts of energy out of our new nit-picker that we are putting into it."

A home without a nit-picker, I always say, is no home at all.

You get the idea: be simple, clear, direct—and as *visual* as possible.

Now you have hooked your listeners by hitting them between the eyes with a tellingly announced topic. To hold them, you must next reveal your three-part plan.

Why? Because if you're going to run a complex movie past your audience's inner eye, you must help listeners by tipping them off to the main skeleton of your "plot." You must implant a neon-lit outline of your script in the listener's head so that he can trace your film through its successive stages.

We'll explain more later about how a listener's mind needs help to follow you through your movie-speech. For now, simply remember that he must get at the outset a bold, sharp photo of your script outline. Just the three major parts: if you hit him with details of subsections, his mind will block from image overkill, and you'll defeat the whole idea of this general tipoff.

Examples? To illustrate how quickly and simply you should flow from defining topic to stating plan, let's place you as a veterinarian telling a convention of colleagues about a deadly new dog disease called anthropophobia:

"Tonight we take from the test-tube an appalling piece of news: not 'man bites dog,' but 'dog hates man.' The canine sickness I shall describe as 'anthropophobia' (or 'AP' for short) should frighten not just postmen and burglars, but every dog-lover in this country.

"And this, for three reasons:

First, the *biological threat:* here I'll tell how the AP virus, while stirring anger in dogs, is also (to dreadful effect) a canine aphrodisiac;

"Next, the *economic threat:* I'll show here how the geometric increase which this hate-aphrodisiac causes in dog population will surpass by thirty-six times our nation's yearly supply of Alpo;

"Finally, the *cultural threat:* here I'll explain how these biological and economic time-bombs may destroy within eighteen months a belief our civilization has cherished for countless centuries: dog as man's best friend." Alpo all gone? Let them eat cake.

In the next example you are a slightly mad scientist, an inventor of mini-computers, who thinks it's time he succeeded in business without really trying:

"You, as potential investors in my mini-computer, have a right to know why it is the best in the world. That's what I'm going to tell you now in talking about:

"First, its *technical superiority:* how it's a full light-year ahead of the competition;

"Then, its *low cost:* how wafers, chips (and cookies?) bring it in at half the cost of its rivals;

"And finally, its *marketability:* how its technical advancement and low cost carve out an enormous new market likely to make all of you—as well as me—stinking rich."

Where do we sign?

One last example to make sure the technique of stating your plan becomes as simple as it is. This time you are a Protestant minister (or a Catholic priest, or a rabbi— pray in the plan of your choice). You are preaching a sermon on the need to be your brother's keeper:

"Cain and Abel said it all: we are our brother's keeper. And when we ask why, three reasons emerge from our dealings, in turn, with our neighbors, ourselves, and our God."

This introduction, about as short as you could make it in stating both topic and plan, plunges in so quickly that the faithful hardly have time enough to wonder how little they'll put in the collection plate. If the sermon or speech is to last less than twenty minutes, you should try to keep your lead-off quite this brief. To convince most people that they are their brother's keeper, you would probably need all the extra time you could get to sock home your arguments anyway.

Warning: never, *never omit to state your plan.* It is your listeners' strongest crutch, their surest defense against your constant rivals: boredom and daydreaming. A quick summary of your scripted plan not only helps listeners track your speech's progress as you give it; it whets their appetite to hear how you will actually pull off the plan.

As a fringe benefit, stating the plan at the start also drills it once more into your own memory. It's a capsule dress rehearsal for the speech you now must deliver—as promised.

The final job your intro should do is to telegraph your conclusion. Already the way you have defined the topic and revealed your trend of thinking in your plan may have hinted at where you're heading. If it has not, you can sharpen your audience's interest by giving a tantalizing glimpse of where you are taking them: "As I sum up the joys of physical fitness, you'll see why the ancient Romans spoke of a healthy mind in a healthy body."

If the topic's nature—a sales pitch for compact cars or some other evangelical appeal—forces you to announce your conclusion baldly at the outset, you must leave the mystery to your argumentation itself. Here the audience's excitement will not come in awaiting an unknown conclusion, but in waiting to see how you get there: "Most of you know that champagne is good for varicose veins. But as I delve into the three main reasons for this, you'll be amazed by the effect of Pommard on fallen arches and by the usefulness of a flirtatious little Chateau d'Yquem in curing several even more intimate problems."

Even *more* intimate than fallen arches? The mind boggles. The audience will stick to you like a lovesick lamprey.

One of the smoothest trainees in this art of elegantly disguised plans and prepared "improvisations" (though a deadly reader of written speeches) is Canadian Prime Minister Pierre Trudeau. On March 24, 1981, he led off a landmark defense of his constitutional policies with a compact and classic little intro.

Watch him cram into three sentences all three functions of a winging-it intro, sliding listeners into a dreary subject with natural grace. In his first sentence he defines his topic: "I realize that *this resolution has caused deep division* among members of both houses of Parliament, members of all political parties, within the ranks of provincial premiers and indeed among the Canadian population." In the second, he states his plan: "However, I find some consolation in the fact . . . that the division seems to arise not so much on the *substance* (part one) of what we are debating as on the *process* (part two) and the *timing* (part three)." In sentence three, he telegraphs his conclusion: *"They are the elements* that are *divisive."*

This is a textbook model, which took him straight into part one and a further statement of plan for part one's subsections: "On the substance, the motion before us poses *two things:* firstly, that *Canada give itself a Canadian constitution with an amending formula* . . . and secondly, the *charter of fundamental rights and freedoms."* He carries on, in typical "Cartesian" form, with the routine reminder of our place in his mind's-eye script: "As for the first factor . . ."

Want to be a prime minister? As Trudeau did in his student days, practice winging it.

Like a gripping introduction, an uplifting, memorable ending should be short, to the point, quotable, and, especially, colorful. As they say in show biz, it should "leave 'em laughin' "—even if the laughin' is cryin'.

To do all this, and to wrap up your finely woven speech with an impression of start-to-finish unity, you should make your ending do two jobs: recall your three-part plan (movement); and focus on a photo of part three (picture).

As you see, we carry the notion of a moving picture right to the end. We just inverted the order—picture before movement—that we followed earlier.

After announcing your plan during the introduction, and following it through the "body" of your speech, you should hammer home its awesome three-part symmetry by restating it concisely at the end—in one to three sentences.

You don't need to do this if your speech is extremely short—say, under five minutes. If you clutter up your speech with too much restating of your plan, you'll end up with all plan and no speech. But normally you will find this brief restatement of your reasoning process a useful tool to sway hesitant listeners to your viewpoint. Assuming your basic three-part argumentation is sound, this final flashback on your logic should seem to the audience—as a "conclusion" should—conclusive.

At the very least you will remind your audience before they file out of the hall that you have an organized mind. They may still think you're nuts. But they'll think of you now as a lunatic with logic. (Since the three-part wrap-up and the final focus are interwoven so intimately, we'll give examples for both together.)

Let's look now at how your end-of-movie focus works. Having run your movie past the audience with vividness and inspired pacing, having wound listeners to a pitch with your three-part wrap-up, now you must do what you often see at the end of a movie at the neighborhood Roxy: freeze the final frame. The final frame, the image you want to burn into your listeners' minds, is simply the major point you proved in Part III about the core-theme.

Again, you need not recapitulate your whole detailed argumentation. The three-part plan reminder you have just sketched out creates all the momentum you need for a powerful windup. All you must do is reduce your part-three point to a digestible formula, a slogan, an image.

This is worth a great deal of care. For the last thing your audience hears ("sees"?) will quite possibly be the only thing they'll remember. A simple trick to psych up for this is to imagine yourself sending the audience out into the world to fight for your cause. This may be peddling peanuts, religion, tax breaks, or transcendental levitation—you want a windup paragraph, and final image, to unleash a mob of dragon-slayers.

This final paragraph and sentence need clarity, aptness, color, emotion. Let's see what we can do in a three-part wrap-up, then a still-shot, with two examples.

In the first, you are a farmer. You have just wowed a fieldful of fellow bean-growers with a three-part stem-winder on how a new bovine fertilizer can boost bean production.

"In demonstrating this breakthrough with cattle dung fertilizer, I've dug into the whole process of bean-growing: planting, nurturing, and harvesting. When you think about this, and when you preach the manure message to your neighbors, just remember one thing: Bullshit brings better beans!"

Some of my closest relatives are farmers. No B.S.

To clean up, or at least deodorize, our act a bit, let's end off with the speech you've always dreamed of giving to the New York Perfume Importers Council. You are the president of the French perfume company that devised the ineffable fragrance called *"Sans Merci"* (very rough translation: "Never Say Thank You"):

"Gentlemen, you have no doubt been astounded to learn of the weeks we needed to plant the acres of fresh flowers contained in even a vial of this liquid enchantment; of the years of sweat we invest in crushing their petals so delicately; and of the centuries of good taste which guide our judgment when we blend them to this perfection. Ponder that, then tell the story thus to the woman you love: *'Sans Merci*—as timeless as you.'" As timeless, though probably not quite as naïve, if she buys that.

Now you have in hand the heart of our little system of made-for-TV-movies speechmaking. You are right to observe that to pull off an apparently improvised speech—I prefer to call it a noteless speech—you have to prepare nearly as much as you do for a fully written and read speech.

It's the *way* you prepare that is different: the noteless speech, paradoxically, needs to be far more soundly structured for you to: 1) remember it, and 2) feel secure and free enough with it truly to improvise the detail en route.

Our guiding principle throughout these past three chapters is the old wisdom of social as well as rhetorical legend:

> *Before you put your mouth in motion,*
> *Get your mind in gear.*

Now that you are geared up with a method, you need to drill it into your guts before you are really ready to fly noteless.

That's what we'll show you how to do in the next chapter. It's homework time—but if you follow instructions, you can make most of it fun and games. Not to mention parties.

The object of oratory alone is not truth, but persuasion.

—THOMAS MACAULAY, "Essay on Athenian Orators"

PART TWO

MASTERING HOW: DRILLS AND DELIVERY

For all a rhetorician's rules
Teach nothing but to name his tools.

—SAMUEL BUTLER

CHAPTER SIX

From Drill to Instinct

Feeling cocky? If you drop this little handbook now to rush back to that gory spy novel, you'll know as much about the principles of on-your-feet improvisation as any two, maybe three, used-car salesmen. But you don't need blood. You need sweat—the sweat of an athlete in training. Stick around, and you'll change the last three chapters of mind-straining rules into effortless instinct.

This Part Two of our book aims to translate the techniques outlined in Part One into second nature for you. The following four chapters will take you from your first run-throughs of winging it right up to the finer points of onstage performance of an actual speech.

Chapter Six starts you off with some mind-stretching drills you can easily make entertaining; Chapter Seven leads you on to some day-of-speech tune-ups; Chapter Eight confides a last-minute checklist on how to get ora-

torically airborne; and Chapter Nine counsels tricks and
trade-offs to avoid crashing.

I won't try to convince you that this leap from theory
to habit is painless. It's tough enough, but mainly as a discipline. You don't have to be an Einstein to get the hang of
winging it. You do need a strong will to banish your onstage shyness.

That's why you're reading this, isn't it?

Like any worthwhile reform of mind or manners,
winging it requires a minimum of perseverence. Just reading this book should take you a long way along the path to
freer, fresher speechmaking. Following through on the
drills offered next will make the system second nature to
you.

Depending on your intelligence, mental rigor, and the
time you put in, you should be able to change yourself
from a fear-frozen bumbler at the lectern to a confident,
engaging speaker in anything from one to three months. If
you plunge in right now with, say, three hours a day on
these drills, you could be in shape for winging a minor
masterpiece of a speech by next week.

You may not be so zealous. If you're as lazy as some
of us are, and habitually postpone work, you'll put in at
most a half hour for a day or two. Then you'll slip into
guilt-ridden little ten-minute sessions once every few days,
finally to drop the whole thing—until the calendar for your
next speech makes you kick yourself in a last-minute
frenzy.

Most readers, I trust, will fit somewhere between the
fanatics and the backsliders. And it is for this serious-but-

unmasochistic majority that I have designed the following tiptoeings through the oratorical tulips.

To help you along, I won't ask you to take tragically my exhortations to plod through rigorous daily drills. For you, as I found most useful for myself, I suggest trying the exercises herein mainly when you feel like it. Ah, the cunning of reverse psychology! I know, and you know, that if you don't feel you're a fink every time you miss your daily dose of Descartes-on-the-teleprompter, you'll think kindly of such a tolerant method—and practice it even more devotedly! Well, we'll see.

To create the right mood for this undisciplined discipline, this do-it-when-you-feel-like-it diligence, you can make this a game. In fact, to make the work work, you must.

You can't shape a habit out of repulsion. You can when "getting there" truly has been fun. You can when the hope of more fun draws you back to game-like rules—rules which prove you can pry your white knuckles off the lectern and sway the groundlings like an old actor ad-libbing poetry.

You think that's all fluff and bluff? Just flash ahead to these subtitles, with words as promising as "random," "scrounging," "nibbling," "instant," "parties," "stealing," and "quickies." They do not mislead. They lead on. So read on.

1. Random Rehearsal

We're trying to get the spirit of winging it flowing through your veins like a nourishing bloodstream. That spirit contains two elements: order and freedom. More precisely, as we have hinted, it is freedom *through* order.

"Order" does not mean you have to slog away at drills with Prussian punctiliousness. It means that when you do practice, you retrain yourself to think with, well, Gallic rigidity.

In the sections following, we'll look at do-it-yourself ways for such training. The point to register first is that to make the fastest, most agreeable progress, you should adopt the habit of grabbing moments for self-instruction at random. Think of winging it *à la française* as your secret sin. Even in the busiest schedules, there's always, always, time for that. . . .

In sum, a chore is a bore. A bit of unscheduled self-development, like Prince Hal's "rare-accident" holidays, should feel like creative leisure.

2. Scrounging for Topics

When you are an accomplished "winger" of speeches, you will display an amazing knack: the ability to take almost any topic, cut to its central issue, then spew out half a dozen outlines (or "plans") for explaining it—all within ten to twenty minutes.

How do we get you from here to there? We can do it by exposing you, helter-skelter, to the broadest array of topics possible. Then we will teach you to seize themes at will, no matter how little you know about them, and we will train you to rattle off the main issue and three or four likely plans that break the topic down and present your viewpoint on it in a convincing way.

Never mind whether you really have a viewpoint on the marble-polishing industry in Rumania. We're retraining you to sound off plausibly on any subject under the sun. To defend any position, any thesis, as long as it exercises your gray cells.

(Have gums, will babble? Perhaps not.)

Where do you get your raw materials for these solo flights at home or office? From newspapers, magazines, radio and TV, your personal library, the things your friends, enemies, and/or family tell you, things you see in your room or out the window, things you imagine, or things you imagine you imagined. Anywhere, anyhow.

Take a randomly selected issue of *Time* magazine (December 8, 1980) as an example. I spy pieces on robots, writers in Tennessee, Sugar Ray Leonard beating Roberto Duran, Poland's trade unions, self-help lawyers, big spenders, a baby ballerina, the sex of God, coffee-table books for Christmas, Jody Powell at retirement, a Los Angeles band called the Bus Boys, and the revival of the ROTC. The periodical presents a buffet of topics to delight the connoisseur of spurious plans.

Try listing themes out of the table of contents of any current magazine. Such general periodicals as *Time* or *Newsweek* are first-class for inventing speech topics. They are up-to-date, are written for "the average intelligent person," and cover a range of topics to rope in gigantic readerships—including highly cultivated people such as you.

Likewise you can lift topics out of TV or radio news bulletins: a strike, an anti-abortion fight, the launching of a ship, the resignation of a Supreme Court judge, an earthquake, an election in Italy.

Or you can skim through the titles (and chapter titles) of books you see around you: James Bond, Mesopotamian architecture, demon cribbage, the poems of Shelley, bayou biology, the physiology of laughter, the intellectual life of the snail.

If none of the above-mentioned virtually inexhaustible sources triggers your creative urges, do something desperate: talk to your family. They will tell you plenty of topics, beginning with the rotten day they had, and ending with the bizarre behavior of a certain other family member who has taken to bugging the others to give him or her something—anything—to think about. Indeed, your present antics would make a marvelous theme—weird, but engaging.

3. Nibbling to the Core

Depending on the time you estimate you have at this or that random moment, jot down five, ten, fifteen, or twenty topics thus gleaned. You don't have to use them all at one sitting. Try a few, then give up when you get either fed up, or drunk with a sense of triumph.

A rule of thumb for developing each drill topic: about six minutes per subject (two to decide what the core-theme should be, four to hatch at least one credible plan). This is a much shorter time than the twenty minutes cited for a core-search in Chapter Three. The twenty minutes are for an actual, real-life speech. Here we just want to drill you—one, two, three, bingo—in quick, intense bursts until you get the routine in your reflexes. Then you can use it confidently in a more probing search.

To remind yourself of a handy way to zero in on the issue at the marrow of your subject, flip back to Chapter Three, to the section "Why and How To Find a Core-Theme First." The system laid out there looks a bit elaborate for these little blitz-drills; indeed, as you get good at cutting to the heart of a subject, you will often be able to do the job without writing anything down. But for now, especially if you're a complete beginner at stump speaking, you may find it quicker and more reliable to put on paper whatever points come to mind.

Remember the trick that tracks you onto some coincidence of interests between you and your listeners: list *your* reactions to the topic, then the *audience's* likely concerns, then *underline words* which you suspect may lead to overlaps, thus to good core-themes.

Let's try a few topics now. You take your own magazine, newspaper, girl friend, lover, enemy, or whatever as *your* source for ideas to delve into. I'll fool around here with a few of the above *Time* pieces to show you how to practice. I won't write everything out in point form again as in Chapter Three. For easier digestion, I'll just free-float some thoughts past you as a narrative. When you core-search your topics, however, you will not bother tacking together sentences; you'll use the point-form, instant-view format outlined at the end of Chapter Three.

We'll start with my own haphazard reactions to ro-

bots, then go on to what two or three imaginary audiences
might think of them. Bear in mind that the following lei-
surely wanderings are my own very personal, shoot-from-
the-hip imaginings. Yours, if you relax and let go, will
prove at least as valid. Don't ape my style of free-floating.
Trust your own values, logic, and wit. You will come up
with ideas and approaches of surprising richness. Best of
all, what you imagine will be *you*—your favorite and most
familiar topic. So let *your* personality flow into all your
themes, and both you and your listeners will sense the result is natural, thus believable.

Now, what the devil do robots do for me? Here goes.
I'll put in italics what seem to me to be promising trigger
words (which you would underline), to highlight likely
overlaps of my interests with those of my audience.

Robots, I suspect, will soon replace dogs as *man's best
friend*. Is that the core issue here? Freeing man from *drudg-
ery*—tedious, repetitive assembly-line work? Or is the
issue *productivity*—helping North American businesspeo-
ple save money on highly unionized wages and better
quality-control in order to compete with those indecently
hard-working, conscientious Japanese, who think that if a
job's worth doing, it's worth doing well?

Or could the issue be workers' increased *leisure* time?
How a two-day work week might drive husbands up the
wall only slightly after they drive their wives up the wall by
bumming around the house watching dumb football games
on TV? Could the issue be the *quantum leaps* of current
technology? Could it be the *impact of such technology* on
social and *political* customs, even on *civil rights* (surely

even robots have the right to go to the bathroom once in a while . . .).

Well, that's what robots do for me. Naturally, the twists you give the topic will mirror not only your own culture, background, and psychology. They will reflect the needs of your imaginary audiences: if you were going to wow a group of *feminists* about the joys of robots, you might mischievously think about how robots *raise the consciousness* of women to the notion that 3CPO and his pals might someday *replace men for everything*. The thought makes me acutely *insecure*, but I suppose science must march on.

You might, on the other hand, ask yourself how you would speak about robots to a class of *high-school students*. One logical angle would be the ways in which robots might *shape careers* in ten or fifteen years.

If you pretended you were talking to a pipefitters *union*, you might examine how robots diminish the joys of extorting sky-high wages through paralyzing, monopolistic *strikes*. If you wanted to flatter the union leaders, you might hint—this has happened in some newspaper printing trades—that unions ought to claim *jurisdiction* over machines and, presumably, collect *dues* for them from their owners.

Solidarity forever? Then pass the oil can, I'm feeling itchy. . . .

Out of the words in italics, you get a clear enough feeling that the key issue with robots has to be their *consequences for human happiness*. Intriguing as robots' guts of wires and light-emitting diodes might be, robots' medium is not their message. The message is us—the fragile, flesh-

and-bone bundles of nerves, emotions, ideas, illusions, and egos known as human beings. The only exception to this human-centered approach to robots, I should think, might be a speech to a seminar of robot repairmen. Even then, you could come out of left field with an ethics-and-screwdriver-rattling angle about robot repairmen, like their counterparts in human medicine, being bound by the Hippocratic oath. . . .

Well, we're straying again. Perhaps that *Time* article on the sex of God is good for a core-search game, too. First, my interest in God's sex, which I assure you is reverential, is indeed imbued with a certain sense of futility; then comes the views of two religious groups, the Transcendental Anabaptists and the Self-Revealing Gerontocrats (the latter more familiarly known as the Flashers . . .).

Personally, ahem, to tell the truth, I have never thought about God's sex with what you might term obsessive fascination. But I'll try. I suppose the main things about God for me are that He's *unprovable*, but highly *plausible* (I am, you see, a Presbyterian agnostic). His existence strikes me as probable not only because of all kinds of *unexplainable phenomena* such as *love* or the *beauty* we see in a pale yellow rose. It now seems almost an article of faith with *mainstream scientists* who peddle the Big Bang theory of the universe: as Robert Jastrow, the Dartmouth College authority on life in the cosmos, has eloquently put this reconciliation of empirical reason and divine belief: "The scientist has scaled the mountains of ignorance; he is about to scale the highest peak; as he pulls himself over the final rock, he is greeted by a band of theologians who have been sitting there for centuries."[1]

The whole supposition of a Big Bang supposes in turn a cause, a universe-starting *authority*. Since this authority rests on unimaginable physical *power,* we are inclined to think of mankind's more *muscular* sex. Besides, I'm a *male chauvinist pig* and it flatters me to think that one of our boys made it to the top. . . .

How might our more professionally religious audiences relate to God's sex? No doubt with alarm. The Transcendental Anabaptists might go for a female divinity on grounds that if you're going to have a second baptism as an adult you want to feel you're sort of back in the *womb.* As self-surpassing high-flyers, they might also reason that God as Woman might have *Her feet more on the ground* than a flightier male version.

The Self-Revealing Gerontocrats? Flashers instinctively reach for a raincoat when they want to reveal their deity's *dignity:* they believe only a *stern Father* would *punish* them by making them parade around in a raincoat, rain or shine.

The *common thread* in both my fantasy and those of our religious friends is *mystery.* Mystery is imagined from mystical and scientific viewpoints. Then, for the two target-audiences, it grows from different psychological needs: the fellows from T.A. plainly crave a mommy-figure; the boys from Aquascutum yearn for Big Daddy.

1. *God and the Astronomers,* New York, W. W. Norton & Co., 1978, p. 116.

Both parent-figures are mysterious not just because of their power, but because, no doubt, of cross-sexual Freudian tuggings. The boyish believer loves yet fears his Earth Mother; the girlish believer tingles at the thought of tender, tough old Pop.

Let's hear it then for *mystery* as our core-theme. We'll now go on to other examples to show you the kind of drills you should try in order to break core-themes down into three-part plans.

We'll mingle "straight" and quirkish examples. Don't knock the nonsensical ones. They help in two ways: by lightening the drill, and by demonstrating, literally in the absurd, that winging it can fit any subject. Both reasons should egg you on—unless you can only learn through suffering.

4. Instant Plans

You should practice the above core-searching drill a few dozen times, until it slips easily to mind each time you take up a topic. Our next job is to drill you in cracking down your core-themes as quickly as possible into usable plans.

Here again the subject matter doesn't matter. It's your mental reflexes we're interested in. Any idea that teaches them to jump when you want them to will suit our purpose.

When you were training yourself above to leap to the heart of each topic, two, five, or ten subjects at a time, you were giving yourself about two minutes per core-search.

Now, for breaking down each topic, give yourself about four minutes a subject.

At first, you will find this hard, perhaps impossible. Remember the old adage that "impossible just takes a little longer." We want to toughen and quicken your mental processes, to channel them within that insufferably rigid "Cartesian" discipline. Try to force yourself along at about four minutes a topic for three or four topics; take a rest with a thin Dutch cigar or a glass of velvety red burgundy, then go back to it. You'll find you're getting the hang of it.

If not, take a day off, buy better cigars and finer burgundy, and this time you'll probably sense you are making progress—to eight minutes per topic, then six, then four. When you are broken in, after a couple of hundred rehearsals of fabricating plans (that's about the ballpark for a breakthrough), you will get your time down to a minute or so.

When you come to doing a real-life speech, you may want to take an hour for plan-shaping. This is the outside limit you should think of, and it should allow you to come up with four or five alternative plans, as we showed in Chapter Four. Then you can pick the best one for you and your audience.

For examples of breakdown drills, I'll take a couple more titles of articles from that old *Time* magazine: Poland's trade unions, and Jody Powell at retirement. This time we'll affect a more serious, but not tragic, tone.

a) *Breakdown into Three-Part Plan:* Our goal here, I remind you, is to take the core-theme apart, then put it back together in a different way that makes sense to you and your audience. As you move from the first to the second to the third part of your plan, you and your listeners should feel drawn along by some measure of forward-moving logic—an "inexorable" force that leads to the conclusion that you want to become the audience's opinion.

Our standards for a sound plan, you will recall, are its ability to simplify (facts and perspectives), illuminate (as images), and advance (your argument). At this stage, you might review the few pages in Chapter Four that explain, step by step, how you carve up a topic into swallowable chunks which follow each other like hors d'oeuvre, main course, and dessert. Then come back to practice a little with the Poles and Jody. So here's a *quick plan-drill* (main outline) for a speech on the Polish trade unions. What we want now—and what you would do in a drill with any topic—is a fast trial-by-error series of potential plans. To get these, we'll take a core-theme which we will pretend to have worked out by our speaker-audience match-up method above. Then we'll try a few obvious formats such as chronological, dialectical (thesis-antithesis-synthesis, or black-white-gray), geographical, and functional. Finally, as you'll recall, we'll ask our conclusion to help us choose the best plan—the one you can argue through best and which the audience should grasp best.

For the sake of argument, let's say we've scanned the interests of both speaker (you or me) and audience (a college-freshman history club) and filtered out as core-theme the notion that history is shaped by personalities, not just economic forces. This theme is a textbook standard among historians. Taking the case of Lech Walesa, the wily, mustachioed little Polish worker in Gdansk who became a worldwide symbol of resistance to Soviet oppression, we can cut the cake several ways. Very quickly, let's try these:

Plan A: Chronological

I. Walesa the boy dreamer
II. Walesa the frustrated worker
III. Walesa the eloquent prophet

This plan, like all chronological ones, offers a neat and instinctive pull forward. It is also extremely easy to remember—our mind being constantly conditioned to think in sequences of time. In a pinch, such as a real "stump" speech where you're given only minutes, or even seconds, to get your mind organized, falling back on a chronological plan is very often the best way to go.

Chronology, however, puts some burden on you to make sense out of a sequence which may have no sense, or not appear to with the time and data you have. If your making sense of time comes off as too contrived or flimsy, your plan will lack analytical power and thought-provoking freshness.

In this Plan A, for example, we are completely sidestepping the issue of economic forces, part of our coretheme. We are snowing our audience with Walesa's colorful life-story. In this sense, critics could accuse us of giving anecdotes, not analysis—of not really answering the question at all.

Let's see how another approach works out.

Plan B: Dialectical

(Thesis-Antithesis-Synthesis)

  I. How a Communist economy shaped Polish thinking
 II. How outstanding individuals (Pope John Paul II and Walesa) triggered freer thinking
III. How, for a time at least, protecting the collectivist economy forced the Communist Party to purge its hard-liners to balance Party control and allow freer expression: a new accommodation between Communist power and the people?

For the reasons given in Chapters Three and Four, the old Hegelian Ping-Pong game of dialectics is fascinating to watch. The forward tension built into its structure can seduce many listeners to the point that they don't really care whether you're speaking wisdom or nonsense: they get their kicks from surfing back and forth on the waves of your plan.

Beware of dialectical plans when you're facing sophisticated audiences. Unless you are deeply certain of your evidence and opinions, they may unmask you as a con artist. That you are, of course—but a con artist is no good at all if the people he needs can see through him. For your college-freshman history club, you could probably get away nicely with a black-white-gray plan. With no offense to the late-teenage mind, the kids you're dealing with would no doubt not know volumes about Poland, and most of them would eat up anything that takes them for a joyride of specious logic.

Those characteristics, I suspect, along with more or less justified rage at economic inequities, probably lie behind the success of Marxism in dozens of intellectually sheltered societies. Just don't try this flashy substitute for truth too often on audiences who have points of comparison in either knowledge or methods of reasoning.

A more cut-and-dried tack takes land as its foundation:

Plan C: Geographical

   I. Northern region (Gdansk) is cockpit of social change
  II. Southern region follows north in historically typical tradition
 III. Individuals have nothing to do with this north-south phenomenon

Here we are putting all our Easter eggs in one basket: the doubtful theory that everything important in Poland starts up north, then trickles down. Because the conclusion it leads us to is so categorical and dicey to prove, I would drop this plan like a bad Polish joke.

One last try, just to see where we might go:

Plan D: Functional

   I. The role of the economy: in shaping any political balance of power (Polish collectivism allows a largely free agriculture)
  II. The role of leaders: in focusing political attitudes (Walesa, in his ideas and style, instantly summed up workers' hopes)

III. Today's Polish crisis draws on both these elements: unlike the monolithic USSR, Poland's "mixed" economy made Poland ripe for a pluralist revolution; Walesa brought timely talents to pick this fruit of freedom

Now, as we explained earlier, the way to choose the best plan is to let your conclusion do the picking. Which of the above outlines strikes you as the most sensible?

I would probably go for the functional one we just did (Plan D), or as second choice, Plan B, the dialectical one. Note, indeed, how closely they resemble each other—a sign that you may be on to basic facts and arguments.

Why choose these plans? First, because both come to satisfyingly clear, sensible, give-and-take solutions. Hints of tunnel vision, of ideological blinkers, tend to unconvince intelligent audiences with reassuring promptness. Common sense should always be your main reason, but a second, back-up reason rests in the forward pull these two plans display. They tug strongly and plausibly to a credible viewpoint.

A final reason comes from the two plans' potential for vividness: they look promising to me as moving-picture shows. Just think of the interplay between Polish farmers and workers, or of weaving allegories around the dialectical twitch of Lech Walesa's mustache!

There you have the three ingredients we cited in Chapter Four for using your conclusion to zero in on the best plan: simplicity, illumination, advancement. The makings of a smash-hit movie—assuming you can work up this "film treatment" or outline into a still simple, still vivid, still dynamic script.

b) *Breakdown into Subsections:* Let's give that a shot with Jody Powell. Our idea here will be to take the three-part plan one step further. We're going to assume we've already picked the three-part skeleton by the means above. Then we'll try to flesh out the skeleton into the bones and muscle of subsections—and, when useful, into sub-subsections.

Just a small warning on further breaking down your plan. Break it down as much as you want, but bear in mind two hazards: 1) the more you subdivide, the greater the risk of straining your audience's ability to follow you; 2) likewise for your ability to remember it all—to "simplify, illuminate, and advance" gets harder as your plan gets more detailed.

Apart from these obvious risks, you should break down your topic as much as you must to make a persuasive pitch. This supposes that you will gear the plan's sophistication not just to how inherently complex the subject is, but to how fancy an analysis you think you need to sway your audience.

My advice is to keep a bias in favor of simplicity. Even if once in a while the bright people in your audience tax you with superficiality, it's far worse to be accused of being incomprehensible. Try to resist byzantine structures for their own sake; go for the heart of things. Show the main arteries, and only as many veins and capillaries as you think your listeners really want to see.

Besides, one person's superficiality is another person's clarity. I'm for clarity: just try to be profoundly shallow. . . . So what follows is a quick plan-drill for a speech entitled "Jody Powell Signs Off." Let's assume that we've settled on a conclusion for Jody Powell along the lines of "nice guys finish first, even when their boss loses a presidential election." This opinion has led us to a three-part main plan that tries to profile Powell's success as the best-liked, most believed White House press secretary since John Kennedy's Pierre Salinger. The plan, a kind of inventory of Powell's personality, moves on a dynamic of deep-to-less-deep. It analyzes his impact as follows:

I. Powell's Values: Decency, modesty, frankness, loyalty;
II. Powell's Intellect: Subtle, crafty (intelligently partisan), a Georgia culture agreeably broadened by the classics; and
III. Powell's Style: Simple, ironic, witty, quotable.

If Powell really lives up to this billing, he is surely as saintly as anyone close to the press can be. Let's see how he, and our main plan, stand up to a more detailed breakdown.

At this point, you should bear in mind that we break down main plans into subsections in exactly the same way we develop our core-theme into a main plan: we jot down a jumble of what we think are pertinent facts, spot sub-core-themes, try two or three mini-plans, then let the conclusions they lead us to help us choose the best subsection plan.

I know that sounds elaborate, but we are spelling out this method in baby-steps right now to make it, as Richard

Nixon used to say, "perfectly clear." Once you get the hang of splitting ideas into instant plans, you can race through this process in minutes, even seconds. For now, we've got to be more specific about how we're proceeding. Like skiing or playing blackjack, once you've made the drill an instinct, you'll fly through the routine. Here's a subsection plan-drill focusing on "Jody Powell's Values."

This should not prove complicated: all you have to do is list the main values that you think sum up this charming man's character. For this breakdown (to violate the rules I just reminded you of), you plainly don't need to fiddle around long with core-theme-searches, five alternate plans, and conclusions that select plans. The main heading—Powell's Values—could be complicated by breakdowns to make a Jesuit salivate, but simple is best, whenever possible. This looks like a great chance to keep it simple.

Your main heading almost irresistibly invites you to list Jody's virtues. This should indeed be your first step. Toss on paper anything from three to ten values you think best sum up the man, then narrow this down to the three, four, or five most basic ones. If you list eight or nine virtues in your speech—Remember the thirteen perspectives on birth-control-for-armadillos in Chapter Three?—you'll lose yourself and your audience. And you're likely to end up with overlaps, such as shading "stubbornness" into "perseverance," or "bluntness" into "frankness." To narrow things down, look for the fundamental, the stand-alone basic stuff: "honesty," then "kindness" (not necessarily overlapping virtues), then "courage," for example.

Let's agree, after shuffling through your initial list of up to ten values, that Powell's values are of such paramount importance to his success that you really want to cite six of them. Once you get over four or five in any classification, you would be smart to look for another, deeper subdivision: say, in Jody's case, values he gleaned from childhood (list two), then values picked up from Jimmy Carter.

DOUBLE-SPLIT SUBDIVISION (EXAMPLE A)

- values from childhood: honesty, kindness
- values from Jimmy Carter: courage, persever-ance, and loyalty

This could work, if you think that the particular audi-ence you're facing would appreciate the distinction be-tween Jody's childhood and Carter's influences. Just for the sake of argument, you could also rejiggle the five values into "soft" and "hard" virtues as follows:

DOUBLE-SPLIT SUBDIVISION (EXAMPLE B)

- "hard" values (Jody the tough guy): courage, perseverance
- "soft" values (Jody the Sunday-school grad): honesty, kindness, loyalty

All things considered, though, I wouldn't complicate matters so much. It seems to me that this sterling gentle-man's virtues could easily stand alone in one simple list. You could learn this list by jotting down, then repeating aloud in some silly jingle, the first letter of each word: *c*ourage, *p*erseverance, *h*onesty, *k*indness, *l*oyalty. Now c-p-h-k-l could very well spell *crazy press hacks know little*. With the enormous esteem you hold for the media, such thoughts should flow easily to mind.

Why the order we used, putting courage first and loyalty last? The first and last virtues on the list are the ones that stick most with your listeners. Citing loyalty last allows you to build a nice little crescendo to the one value that gave Powell his greatest strength (Carter's confidence) and greatest weakness (Jody's ill-advised harassment of Senator Charles Percy when Powell rushed to defend accused-of-scandal Bert Lance).

You should play each of the other two main headings according to whichever substructure best fits the material. In other words, having a personal-analytical overall plan does not mean you have to build your sub-plans on a personal-analytical standard too. You could just as well use a geographical or dialectical plan for either of the second or third main sections—always depending on the usual three measuring sticks of a good plan to carry you along: What best *simplifies?* What best *illuminates?* What best *advances* your argument?

Vividness and forward movement might not leap out at you from these abstract values of honesty and loyalty. The way you test these virtues against our benchmarks is by looking at them for the telling detail or anecdote which casts light and color on the core-theme, or which tempts you on to the next point. Can you illustrate Jody's honesty by claiming that he invariably paid back borrowed cigarettes, or only lied (as with the U.S. hostages in Iran) when lives were at stake? Can you bring home his loyalty by recalling that he put out a short-story-length memoran-

dum to clear Hamilton Jordan when Ham allegedly poured
Amaretto down a young lady's blouse in a public bar?

(As Sir Thomas Beecham said when an elephant forgot himself onstage during a performance of Berlioz's
Roman Carnival: "Frightful manners, splendid judgment"
—about the Amaretto.) Following is a subsection plan-
drill on "Jody Powell's Intellect."

Never having met this man, I can't tell you how his
head ticks. But since we're playing a game here, we can
reasonably distill a few traits from his deft handling of
journalistic Draculas: subtlety, craftiness, a sense of headline, a Georgia culture lifted by some acquaintance with
the classics.

How would you place such characteristics? Would you
combine some of them as one (say, subtlety and craftiness)? Could you spot some logical order to list them in a
single inventory—basic to less-basic, broad to narrow, serious to less-serious, general to specific, predictable to un-
usual? Any of these listings might help your listeners make
more sense of Powell's mind.

Let's try a couple to see where they take us in example
A: Empirical: Facts-to-Judgment.

- Sense of headline (how Jody could instantly see
  any problem as the press would see it)
- Craftiness (how he responded to crises by pre-
  cooking headlines by means of very "political"
  responses)
- Subtlety (how he caught local nuances in his PR
  counterattacks)
- Georgia overlay of culture (how political imagery
  and tricks of southern state politics helped him)

● General culture (how, in fact, all his success
  rested on his wide reading)

I don't find that this listing interprets Powell either
manageably or convincingly. It's too long and too contrived and therefore not very persuasive: it's form for its
own sake, not form that focuses. Let's try another way in
example B: Broad-to-Narrow Listing.

● Solid general culture
● Georgia overlay
● Subtlety-Craftiness (combined)
● Sense of headline

This may not overwhelm your audience by it origi-
nality. But it does offer a nice hint of chronological movement, as well as greater simplicity in its linking of subtlety
and craftiness. It's also easy to remember: you start with
the fundamental fact of Jody's broad culture, narrow it a
bit more to Georgia, embrace his allegedly central trait of
subtlety-craftiness, then pinpoint this in the practical skill
of political thinking that made Powell so useful to Carter.

I think this one will do. To lock it in your memory,
use either the trick with key first letters (c-g-s-h for culture, Georgia, subtlety, headline), those key words themselves, or, if you wish, the key-word initials in some silly
phrase: "Colonel Golden's sullen hell-raising." Try each
way to see which one is easiest for you. Then put the cho-
sen words or initials on your mental teleprompter by jotting them on paper and repeating them a few times out
loud.

In fact, in all this chapter's later exercises, that's how

you should roll Descartes onto your mind's-eye teleprompter. This second part of your new discipline is as important as Descartes himself: if you cook up a sparkling
three-part plan but forget to imprint it on your mind-
screen, you will indeed forget it. You will wing it not like a
swallow but like a barnyard goose caught in an oil spill.

What about Powell's style? I thought you'd never ask.
Taking the four adjectives we thought of above—simple,
ironic, witty, quotable—I suggest we latch onto "quotable"
as our target conclusion. After all, if a press secretary can't
get quoted, what good is he?

At close range, I don't see any natural rhyme or
rhythm for splitting these four ideas into groups of two. I
could see dropping "simple" as part of "quotable," but on
balance, I think we should seize this end-of-speech timing
to work up to a pleasingly long crescendo—to end with a
flourish. We can, of course, split any one of the four ideas
into two or more examples: these, especially if colorful,
should lighten your points and make them more graphic.

For instance, in this example of a single-list subsection
with a second-tier split, on the subject of Jody Powell's
style:

- Simple: Being understood is the highest virtue.
  (Jody tells Uncle Remus stories, he leaves six-
  syllable words to preachers.)
- Ironic: A self-deprecating style is the key to
  likeability. (Jody's "aw shucks" shtik charms
  press cynics; his cowboy boots signal informal-
  ity.)
- Witty: Laughter disarms critics, and combines

simplicity and irony (Jody's joke about Rosalyn
as steely-eyed ruler of the western world).

• Quotable: These three approaches add up to a
guy who can get his boss's message across.
(That's what press secretaries are for; that's why
Powell succeeded and "finished first.")

All the above shakedowns and breakdowns look terri-
bly complicated. They are not. You just have to get the
trick of it, then practice, practice, practice. Relax your
mind now until the end of this chapter, and soak up some
tips for helping you program instant plan-making into your
subconscious.

5. Plan "Parties"

One fast way to master the game of instantly breaking
down a topic is to get a friend or two hooked on this game.
Tell your friends how to use the step-by-step method
outlined here. Then agree to work together on surprise
topics.

I can recommend two ways of doing this. You should
try both of them in a congenial, relaxed atmosphere; I shall
leave the choice to your imagination and the texture of
your friendship.

One way is for both (or more) of you to take five
minutes at the outset of your little session and write down a
dozen or so random topics—absolutely anything you
and/or your pals care about: parachute jumping, commodity futures on the stock market, natural childbirth, video-

cassette recorders, office architecture, beauty contests, nuclear fission, love poetry, German music, mortgage rates,
teaching by computer.

Next you exchange your lists. You tell your partners
to take five minutes to pick two or three topics they like.
Then you each take ten minutes, simultaneously, to work
up convincing plans for your topics. After this work time,
you take turns reading off your plans (including alternates,
if any), with each of you asking the others for comments
and criticism.

The blind leading the blind? No. The eager inspiring
the enthusiastic. If you do this in a good, happy spirit of
friendly emulation, you can help each other tremendously.
Just criticize each other with your own native common
sense. Insist that your plans, and your partners' plans,
stand or fall on how *clear, convincing,* and *coherent* they
are. To guide you in your judgments, go back to our old
benchmarks: what *simplifies,* what *illuminates,* what *advances* your argument?

After a few exercises of reading your plans aloud—
our game to nail down Descartes—you can graduate to rehearsals in which you burn your three-part plans (and later
their subsections) onto your memory-screen, then rattle
them off by heart. Descartes on your teleprompter: now
you're drilling your mind both to *think* in a new way and
to *speak* with a new noteless confidence. That's what you're
paying for in this book's subtitle, isn't it?

Don't take any of this tragically. Don't take it literally.
Take it seriously. But have fun—laughter can and should
oil the machinery of learning. If your plan concludes that
every orange-haired jaywalker deserves the death penalty,
that's okay. Just make the traffic-stopping felons zigzag

surely and gracefully through your plan en route to the electric chair.

Another way is to do all the above, but picking your topics from neutral ground such as books and magazines you see lying around. This technique, which we used earlier with *Time*, adds a little excitement and authority to the exercise—you are, after all, now using "real" topics which somebody already thought important enough to write about. It also drums into your head the notion that, once mastered, this instant plan-making can fit any subject under the sun. You can almost feel your confidence surge as you take a solid theme, then cough up a pretty creditable plan.

Be careful, or you'll start to swagger. But why not? We're fighting shyness, are we not?

6. Stealing Practice

Like stolen fruit, unplanned plan-making can prove even more savory than these semiformal "parties" with your pals. What I'm urging here is seizing any moment you find yourself at loose ends, and making it into a private tutoring session. Anything from two to twenty minutes is worth grabbing and using to cook up an instant plan to train your mind.

I've found such moments as waiting for a bus or an appointment good times for this. If it's an appointment, you can exploit the subject matter of the appointment to exercise your mind—this might even help you in the meeting.

At the bus stop (or walking along the street, or

shaving, or whatever), you can take absolutely anything that flits across your mind or eyesight, and chop it quickly into a plan. Cars? A moving subject: past, present, and future; size, mechanics, comfort; European, Japanese, American. Telephone poles? Electrifying: size, shape, function; wooden, steel, cement (with merits and dangers of each). Policemen? Some fast-draw breakdowns: FBI, state, local; traffic, crime, morality; uniformed, detectives, civilians; legal, security, and information aspects.

Are you at the breakfast table, and find your mate hogging the morning paper? Try a spicy little discourse on saltshakers: salt as mineral, as condiment, as myth; the esthetics of saltshakers from Benvenuto Cellini to Queen Victoria to Safeway. No doubt you could muse on the chemical, nutritional, and gastronomic delights of that egg sulking on your plate—not to mention small, medium, and large eggs, or eggs from chicken, geese, and ostriches.

If we're going to make you a knee-jerk three-part Cartesian, we've got to make plan-making a pervasive, if not obsessive, discipline in your life.

You might keep some areas sacred from this quirky bit of game-playing—for instance, the boudoir—though even there, if you're in the mood to giggle, you might make it serve. Before, during, and after?

7. Volunteer Quickies

All of this will come to little but private joy unless, early in the game, you take a public risk or two. After even a week or so of playing the drills we've suggested, you ought to pluck up your courage, look for some modest occasion to try your new three-part wings, and fly. This could be merely an office meeting with three or four trusted colleagues. It could be a brief sales report to your regional manager. It could be a talk to your history class reporting on a new biography. It could be a no-big-deal pitch to your condo council in favor of buying earthquake insurance.

The idea is to start off with low-risk situations, where nothing very scary is at stake. Flap your new wings in larger and dicier situations as you go along. Work up your confidence and technique until you can handle anything up to the toughest audience you're ever likely to meet. If you really buckle down to making joyful madness with this method, you'll quickly see the method in the madness of all this splitting, rejiggling, and game-playing.

Make a point soon of jumping off a small oratorical cliff. Volunteer for little leaps into the blue sky of your imagination, and you will be surprised. You will falter, but you will fly.

Now let's fly beyond practice. Let's veer close to some ways you can pull off a full-scale, white-knuckle flight into noteless eloquence.

What is the short meaning of the long speech?

—SCHILLER

CHAPTER SEVEN

The Real McCoy

All this time, you've been idling your engines, tuning up your technique. Finally you're ready to fasten your safety belt and rev up your motor-magic for a fly-or-flop takeoff. This chapter aims to run you through the paces of immediate pre-podium preparation. We'll take for granted you have already drilled yourself in this winging it method until it's second nature to you. We'll assume you have already worked out a theme for a real-life situation. And we'll suppose you have already hit on a three-part plan you think will positively mesmerize with its inner logic and shimmer with vividness. Well . . . you hope it will work.

At this stage—the very day of your speech, or no earlier than the night before—you need to follow three last-minute steps. If you know your subject and your audience, you are almost guaranteed to make a solid speech. In turn, they will lock in your self-assurance by stretching a safety net under your improvisation; lock in the illusion of ordered eloquence by starting and ending off your talk brightly; and lock in the structure of your talk—which underpins both confidence and eloquence—by distilling your plan down to a simplicity even an amnesiac could hang on to.

Why do this only hours, very few hours, before you risk your favorite ulcer onstage? Because we want to give you the best chance possible to remember where you're going, and how. If you get stage-ready too soon, you may lose sight of your mind's-eye teleprompter by the time you talk. Worse, you'll lose the deliciously stimulating terror of last-minute stage fright, and never learn sink-or-swim discipline: this is born only of your will to survive—indeed, marshal—panic.

On, then, with our three day-of-talk rules: list your headings, draft your opening and closing, and take some dry runs into your subconscious.

1. List Your Headings

What is this? *Writing* out stuff when you're supposed to be winging it? Yes. Not because you intend ever to read your titles onstage. But because the exercise of jotting down headings can help you (again!) in three ways.

First, writing out your skeleton plan helps to reveal fallacies or weaknesses you may have missed in the detailed breakdown of your subject into core-theme and full plan. It's amazing how many worthwhile improvements you can make in your headings, examples, and even witticisms by letting a plan marinate for a day or two, then turning back to it under the emotional klieg lights of the D-Day performance.

Second, writing out your final plan again enables you to simplify it to just the right degree for ready recall. Your battle-ready instincts will tell you how much you need to boil down your plan to remember it most easily. Earlier, when you struggled to break down your topic exhaustively —with subsections and sub-subsections—you tried to weave a rich tapestry. Now, as the moment to explain the tapestry arrives, you will find it natural to omit nuance in favor only of the tapestry's most striking patterns.

Example: in a speech reviewing twentieth-century painting, you have a main heading entitled "Why Modern Art Assaults the Psyche." You might originally have listed under this heading four subsections entitled "Formal Chaos," "Unmatching Color," "Erratic Movement," and "Mood of Despair." Under each subsection you might have grouped two to five points, all in an internal harmony you plainly don't see in modern art.

For your last glance at your plan, you may find it hard to recall these eight to twenty sub-subsections in the right order, if at all. After reading them half a dozen times intensely and repeating them aloud, though, you could drop the sub-subsections from the final plan you feed into your mental teleprompter. Then, if you miss some of the sub-subsection nuances, at least you will impress your listeners with your orderly approach by recalling the main headings.

You are setting priorities—ruthless, speech-saving priorities.

Anyway, if you get lost, just tell 'em that like Tom Wolfe in *The Painted Word,* you think modern painting is a fraud, but you know what you like.

The third reason to jot down a bare-bones plan is psychologically vital: a short, simple plan stuffed in your pocket while you are onstage makes you feel safe. Even though you have no intention of looking at your plan, its presence in your pocket, shoe, or bosom will do wonders for your sense of security. Secretly, a little shamefully, but oh-so-consolingly, you are reassured to know that in a pinch you've got a real-life, not imaginary, "teleprompter."

Not having any bosom worth mentioning, I always stash my last-minute plan in a shirt or jacket pocket. To make sure it doesn't turn out to be more of a nuisance than a help in a blank-minded fix, I always shrink my plan to one sheet of paper, preferably even an envelope. Less, indeed, is more. If ever—God forbid—you should face a total, sudden memory blank, you cannot afford to paw through half a dozen pages to find your place.

Think of this hidden-away envelope, card, or page as your parachute. You never expect to use it. But as you solo elegantly through the thin air of noteless speech, your pocketed little secret will keep you calm. By lurking at hand, your plan makes itself unnecessary. It makes your confidence and paperless eloquence a self-fulfilling prophecy.

Obviously, if you are winging a very short spiel—anything from three to five minutes—you don't need to fiddle long with such a rigmarole. But knowing you've at hand a brief, clearly written summary of headings, with underlined and numbered titles, will allow you to sail serenely through any public trial from the three-minute office presentation to a six-hour Fidel Castro–type epic.

Just take less time, need we say it, for the short talk. Even thirty seconds invested in sketching a plan for the ultra-brief talk can make all the difference. It won't be a silk parachute with all the trimmings; but it will be a parachute —a no-lose secret weapon for your self-assurance.

2. Draft Your Opening and Closing

To disillusion you further about the magic of this "noteless" speechmaking, here's another bit of cheating. It's based on the much-observed superficiality of the collective mind—your audience, however smart or well educated it may be.

The chemistry of oratory enables any halfway clearheaded, fairly well-informed person to sway an audience of individuals with higher knowledge of a given subject. By holding the initiative of speech (not counting eventual hecklers or question-askers), an experienced speaker can time the ebb and flow of listeners' emotions. He can trigger chains of imagery, unleash crescendos and decrescendos of ideas by the sheer clarity and cadence of his discourse.

Not to show contempt for anybody—but to cheer you up—as long as you start and end stylishly, and convey some semblance of orderly thought in the body of your talk, 90 percent of any given audience will be convinced that you've pulled off a first-rate speech.

By schooling you in the disciplined delights of Descartes, we've armed you with a method for at least *sounding* organized in the body of your speech. You may feel as confused about your topic as you always were. But if you've come up with a defensible viewpoint and a plausibly marked path to justify it, you will strike your audience as lucid, even if disastrously wrong.

What you must do to gild this oratorical lily is tack on, front and back, a few lines of provocative prose with overtones of poetry. In short, you need a punchy line or two to kick off your intro, and to round off, with flags snapping and trumpets clamoring, your conclusion.

Cheating again on your "noteless" bluff, you ought to write these sentences out, then memorize them. Memorize? Even if you were jumpy enough about losing your way on-stage to buy this book—you must be bright enough to learn a sentence or two of your own heart-lifting words. Well, start with a couple of very short ones, then work up to five or ten words each.

Why bother chiseling out your most arresting, most ringing eloquence at start and finish? Because first and last impressions are critical. The first words you utter will tell the audience whether or not it—really wants to tune its mind and emotions to you; the last ones will confirm to listeners whether or not you have satisfied them. Like a good meal, it's often the hors d'oeuvres and dessert, the approach and final flourish, that define what really happened—by predisposing, then completing the seduction.

I recall making speeches in which I thought I had delivered the body of the talk with enough rigor and authority to convert a vegetarian to Big Macs. Then, glowing with

pride at how clever I was, I blew the finale: the speech
—limped to an end, trailing off in an anticlimax. On
other occasions, I waited for onstage inspiration to plow
in interestingly. It did not come, and I—wandered into
the subject as my audience dreamed of wandering out of
the hall.

Inspirations do come, and will come more and more
as you grasp the key principle of winging it: do not leave
decisive things to chance. Spontaneity grows from self-assurance. Our cardinal rule for winging it is: *In order to improve, you must prepare.*

Don't think of your start and finish as "mere cos-
metics." As even Sophia Loren will tell you, fine features
need highlighting: your oratorical high cheekbones are
your plan. The soundest structure needs a little embellish-
ment to make it, and you, stand out.

This lesson has shaped the style of all masters
throughout history. Bossuet, legendary French preacher of
the court of Louis XIV, once took a bet (which saintly
souls thought blasphemous) to begin a sermon with three
then-shocking "swear" words: "Jesus, Mary, Joseph." He
did so, startled his sleepy audience into alertness, then went
on to deliver one of his anthology-bound classics, using the
"blasphemies" as his plan. Mark Antony—at least as para-
phrased by Shakespeare—grabbed his listeners by their
togas and cut to the core of his theme with: "Friends,
Romans, countrymen, lend me your ears; I come to bury
Caesar, not to praise him."

As famous last words, one can cite many liltingly
cadenced perorations. Pericles, consoling the widows of ancient Athens' warriors, wound up with: "This is the crown

and prize which (Athens) offers, both to the dead and to their children, for the ordeals which they have faced. Where the rewards of valor are the greatest, there you will find also the best and bravest spirits among the people. And now, when you have mourned for your dear ones, you must depart." As catharsis, as heart-embracing, grief-shattering release, his words were commanding.

Dozens of approaches can work as start or finish. For "starters," you may consider a fable—if it's truly apt and attention-seizing. A very short, to-the-point story can sometimes launch you well. But stories tend to meander, and the purpose of any introduction is to get you and your audience quickly into a clearly defined topic. Never, never use gratuitous jokes. Starting with a rib-tickler unrelated to your theme marks you as an amateur, a trifler scared by both topic and audience.

Other start-off techniques include a question, or series of questions, echoing the audience's likely fears and hopes about your topic: "Why are we fighting the government's new taxes? Where were our representatives when the tax went through? How can we best strike down this outrageous discrimination?" Such sit-up-and-take-notice queries take you and your listeners to the heart of the government's folly. In this case, your three questions may not bring down the government, but they could get you handily into your plan.

Another opening is to baldly state your topic. To catch your audience's ear, you should encapsulate your subject almost as a slogan or proverb—dream up a statement that you think would not look bad carved in stone on somebody's monument. With luck, the monument will be your speech: "Fish are the world's richest, most-neglected form of protein. They are health, sanity, renewal, life itself. If we don't wake up to this soon, we'll be eating Kentucky Fried Chicken until the end of time." Well, Colonel Sanders wouldn't have minded that last part on *his* tombstone. . . .

Speaking of fish, which we were not, really, your first words must aim to fly-cast a line straight into your listeners' curiosity. You must strike your fish-listeners quickly and accurately, then reel them in throughout your speech. Each transition to a new subsection, each vivid example, each memorable phrase or tension-relieving witticism, jerks the line again. Your fish, by nature, think of nothing but escape: if your bait tastes lousy, or if you leave your line lax, they will get away—to slumber, to the bar, or to a better speaker in the hall next door.

In a good speech, the audience is always asking itself: What's next? You must lead listeners on, or they will chase you off.

The same punchiness, if a different psychology, prevails at the end of your talk. Here you're trying to round off your topic so that listeners will leave agreeing that you have at least a credible case. At best, you are striving to send your audience back to the world outside, as we have argued, to slay a dragon or two; at modest least, you hope listeners will have softened their disgraceful biases toward your truths.

Again, potential round-offs for your conclusion are, not to make a bad pun, endless. Plainly, the one you choose, just as for your introduction, should fit the topic and your treatment of it to perfection. Unity of mood is vital: you can't make a sober-sided case for legalizing pot, then blow it all up in sickly smoke by trotting in some cutesy joke in your last sentence. You can end whimsically, but you should telegraph your whimsy earlier in the game. Otherwise, you will sound disjointed and inconsistent, or just plain mixed up.

One technique to avoid is that of completely recapitulating your ideas. We are dealing here only with a few words of flourish to focus, illuminate, and lift a conclusion already solidly drawn.

A couple of examples? I like a soft-voiced crescendo of hammer-blow phrases using the same rhythm. Here your cadence strengthens your point, which should emerge in simple, evocative words. Sliding obliquely from Colonel Sanders to Dr. Tarnower, let's dally with diets: "These, then, are the pillars of sensible nutrition: chew little, chew slowly, chew not what you want but what you need."

That'll give 'em plenty to chew on. Animal fats excepted, of course.

In the dragon-slaying department, you might also point a final finger at your *bête noire,* and hand the folks a little road map and sword: "The culprit is bureaucracy. The way to tame it is ballots. And you and I, my friends, are going to stuff those ballots where they'll do the most good. . . ." Mmm, perhaps we could work on that, but you get the idea.

One of the best wind-up men around is President Ronald Reagan. Remember his TV debate with Jimmy Carter? The one a withering wit termed a victory for Grecian Formula over Ultra Brite? Whatever you think of Reagan's politics or hair color, you must admit he narrowed millions of pairs of eyes to judge the most Jimmy-hurting issues in his summing-up singsonging of five close-to-Main-Street questions:

> *"Are you better off than you were four years ago? Is it easier for you to go and buy things in the stores than it was four years ago? Is there more or less unemployment in the country than there was four years ago? Is America as respected throughout the world as it was? Do you feel that our security is as safe, that we're as strong, as we were four years ago?"*

Strong stuff. And this was only the wind-up, reminding people why they should vote against Jimmy Carter. Reagan went on to end on a positive note by telling voters why they should vote for him. By summarizing his own candidacy in one all-encompassing promise to free people from bureaucrats and taxes, Reagan finished brilliantly. His two final sentences made Americans sense that he and they could change things together, that he would channel their energies to a freedom and greatness which, by implication, the Democrats had stifled:

> *"I would like to have a crusade today, and I would like to lead that crusade with your help. And it would be one to take government off the backs of the great people of this country, and turn you loose again to do those things that I know you can do so well, because you did them and made this country great."*

Call it chintzy, vague, and maudlin if you wish, but it worked. It left listeners with a simple, powerful message:

"Vote for me and you'll feel good about yourself and your country."

Reagan's wind-up, even with its characteristic folksy awkwardness, is a classic illustration of what the ancient Roman master Crassus said of endings in Cicero's first essay *On the Orator:* "And finally, there should be a peroration, to amplify and reinforce all the points which support one's own arguments, while invalidating and demolishing those that favor the other side."

Crassus, as cited approvingly by Cicero, likewise argued for well-prepared introductions. "Before passing to the actual substance of the speech," he decreed, "one ought to pronounce a preamble aimed at winning the audience's goodwill." You'll find the same advice ringing through the counsel of the ages' most stirring speakers: polish your start and finish, and a well-shaped argument will take care of itself.

3. Dry Runs into
Your Subconscious

So you've got a plan with a dazzling core-theme and a structure to rival the symmetry of the pyramids. You have written out your beginning and ending as compactly carved and graceful bookends to your pleading. How, now, do you reel your spiel onto your mind's-eye teleprompter?

The time you take depends enormously on the length, difficulty, and importance of your proposed speech. You may add or subtract minutes to match your skills, but you ought to aim at spending no more time loading your memory-teleprompter than the planned length of your talk. Thus you would take one hour to ingest the plan, preamble, and wind-up of a one-hour speech; fifteen minutes for a quarter-hour talk.

Isn't it foolhardy to use so little time? No, not once you get the hang of this technique. Not once you gain the audience-tested confidence to trust how alert a last-minute memory-blitz can make you.

Remember, we are talking here of what you do the very day of your speech—preferably even the last half-day before it. You structured your plan much earlier; now you are just imprinting its outline on your invisible teleprompter. You are putting your titles in lights, ready for projection on an imaginary screen during your talk.

Leaving this final write-up until minutes before you go on makes sense on three counts.

First, it keeps the plan, and your opening and closing pyrotechnics, fresh in your mind. Second, this deliberately short time-span prevents you from worrying yourself into a funk—Parkinson's Law (work expands to fill the time available for it) gnaws at the nerves as surely as it squanders your energy. Third, you save time for other psyching-up activities, which may do you more good than rattling off your plan thirty times more.

Such activities, as we shall argue next chapter, should always include infiltrating your audience, if you do not already know it eyeball to eyeball. They should include anything that relaxes you, such as a spot of yoga (in a hotel room, putting your feet on the wall gives you a breath-taking view of the ceiling), pacing up and down, smoking whatever helps, snatching a very measured drink, touching your toes, swinging from the chandeliers—or talking casually with someone other than yourself.

Yourself you should talk to firmly and eloquently by repeating aloud your plan, preamble, and ending as often as you can stomach. First you read, then you recall. Just try to imagine your whole speech outline rolling past your eyes on a screen that's always straight in front of you, even when you turn your head. Imagine that at the back of your head a powerful, fail-safe projector is running the whole script past your eyes onto this screen. You'll see how easily this works in the next two chapters.

If the image flickers or fades, backtrack your projector and roll through the same passage three or four times. Then run the whole script through (verbatim for the start and finish, in quick outline for the plan) until you miss no major points and can replay it at will.

All this time you are repeating aloud what you see on your secret teleprompter. After a few rickety, nervous tries, you'll get it. Your projector will get more and more reliable; your screen will get clearer.

Obviously, you are not going to listen to my advice to do this only at the last minute. You are going to cheat and rehearse a day or a week ahead. Fair ball for beginners— why should you risk this cliff-hanging nonsense first time out before a real audience?

But after you've done your early-bird preparations, do this last-minute push too. You must get into the habit of mastering and channeling the tensions which we all feel just minutes before we speak. As you pull off one or two half-decent "improvised" speeches, you can trust yourself more and more to perform under pressure, and drop the panicky, too-early warm-up. Stage fright, as we showed earlier, can become your best friend. It can sharpen your wits, keep you on your toes, stir you to surpass by far your long-presumed averageness. Creative terror: learn to love it, and you'll start to be a pro.

Here's a refinement you will find helps build this creative tension: as zero-hour approaches, shorten the parts of the plan you repeat aloud to just the main headings. In a crunch, that is, in a sudden blank, you'll have a far better chance of hanging on to the thread of your argument if you can summon up at least the essentials. If you forget a sub-subsection of Part III of your talk, few will notice. If you completely forget Part II (as I did once) you will gasp for words like a beached barracuda.

The same shorten-to-remember rule applies to your intro and your ending. If you find, as the clock ticks down to your grand entrance, that you simply cannot recall all those "unforgettable" words you made up to entice—then dismiss—your listeners, cut down your start and finish to something briefer. Better one strong sentence that you can remember and deliver confidently than three that you mess up through nervousness.

Play your rehearsals of start and finish for an Academy Award. This may call for subtlety or a Reagan-type crusade; it may call for a whisper or a shout. Just keep it classy and keep it apt. Make it fit you, your topic, and your audience. Then you will thrive. If you are as big a ham as most of us are, you can probably even make your listeners forget that your argument is full of holes.

A final word on transitions. Between your plan's main parts and subsections, it may often prove helpful to slot in an apropos phrase or witticism to move your screenplay forward smoothly. You may want to slip this into your last-minute blitz as well. As you cultivate a natural manner in a few well-received speeches, these lubricating words will creep in on their own as you speak.

They may be as simple as a "So much for that," "What can we draw from this?", or "If you can't buy that argument, try this one, which proves the opposite." They may be more elaborate, with wit to fit theme and listeners. But even if banal, they make for an easier-sounding flow than a mere mechnical enumeration.

You will have to experiment with these devices yourself. People's talents, training, and experience vary so much, as do topics, that no rule on transitions can suit everybody.

A fine model for exploring such well-rehearsed detail is Alistair Cooke, that suave and "spontaneous" presenter of PBS's "Masterpiece Theater." Cooke—in my view the smoothest, most watchable man on TV—confesses to memorizing his spiels right down to each engagingly British swallow, pause, and grope for a phrase.

Remember your goal: to throw away your debilitating *visible* crutches, and to concentrate artlessly on the liberating *invisible* support that your plan is. As soon as you can, start to trust yourself. Take the intelligent risks that a person who knows his subject and argument can, then try to fly. To paraphrase Reagan, we are aiming to get paranoia off your back, and to turn you loose to become a great speaker. That should not even take you four years.

The applause of a single human being is of great consequence.

—BOSWELL, *Life of Johnson*

CHAPTER EIGHT

Six Tricks for Takeoff

Time to get really sneaky. By now you've done your home-work for a solidly structured "spontaneous" speech. In the minutes before you take the spotlight, right up to the moment you start speaking, you can do lots more to ensure a smooth takeoff.

This little checklist of common sense does not include that classic bromide of white-knuckle flyers: a wee nip of something medicinal. The proper dosage of tippling—to calm the nerves without causing you to trip over the plat-form—demands another chapter, for which we have no space.

But keep the facts of your own physiology in mind. If you need a snort of something before you can face your friendly lynch mob, make it light, make it little, make it last. And if you have any left over, just send it on to my publisher. He and I will put it to honorable use some time when we are *not* making a speech.

Bear in mind the healthy alternative to chemical courage: real confidence comes from knowing your job, from having done your homework. Your job—a sensible, persuasive speech—should rest on a solid plan and preparation, then on techniques that keep you in control of yourself, your ideas, and your audience.

We'll look now at some such techniques that usually work. The little tricks I'll mention may strike you as just plain old good sense. But when panic takes over, as it sometimes does for the stage-bound, good sense often gets crowded out. Forgive me for stressing the obvious. It's for a fine cause: remaking you into a modern-day Cicero. Here you are. Take what you need, and pride yourself on knowing the rest.

1. Infiltrate Your Audience

I don't want to spoil a useful point with an off-putting example, but the guy who made this a science was Adolf Hitler. Experts agree with Marshall McLuhan that Hitler would have bombed on TV. Too "hot" for a "cool" medium, too loud and flamboyant for living-room intimacy, he would probably have faded fast on television as a comic upstart.

If you've seen films of a Nuremberg rally, though, you know that Hitler was a genius at moving a mob to hysteria, then at lifting and lowering it, just as a great conductor sways a symphony orchestra. As a technician of crowd

control, Hitler knew his stuff—to mankind's ultimate horror. No doubt you can graft his efficiency onto a better
cause.

Before any major speech, Hitler made a point of mixing briefly with "ordinary" members of his audience. He
did not stick only with Nazi Party bigwigs; he tried to look
into the eyes of random spectators, even to exchange a
word of small talk to hear some echo or emotional intonation. This practice, he found, allowed him to take his audience's "temperature"—to get a feel for its mood, its needs,
its expectations. Even with a mainly written speech, he
would then adapt his pitch, his rhythm, sometimes even his
phrasing, to what he read in those eyes or heard in
snatches of talk.

You may not be playing Nuremberg every day, but
the idea of plugging into your future listeners' minds and
psyche before you take the mike should become an easy
habit. If not done obviously or mechanically, it can get you
more quickly into your listeners' trust, and stiffen your own
confidence right from the start of your speech.

Since you may be facing audiences ranging from two
people to two thousand or more, naturally you have to act
accordingly in rubbing shoulders before opening your
mouth. If your audience is very small, chances are you will
be drawn by the very smallness of the meeting room into
chatting with, or locking eyes with, three or four people before you go on. If you are to face a crowd in the hundreds
or thousands, you may have to go out of your way a bit.

How, exactly, can you get closer to big audiences before speech time? By politely asking your official hosts on
the inviting committee to leave you alone for a few minutes

or half an hour. The purpose is to escape the often superficial, jokey, protocol-heavy chitchat your official pilots usually feel obliged to drag you into—with all good intentions—to put you at ease.

The only way you will find peace of mind is by knowing you are on target with your message. So tell your hosts that you would like to pull your thoughts together one last quiet time. Respectful of your imminent ordeal, they will invariably leave you alone. Then it's up to you to "infiltrate" your audience.

I've found two ways to do this. If, as I think is desirable for a big convention-type speech, you arrive the night before you speak, you can pick up a fantastic feel for your potential victims by getting yourself invited to one or two well-chosen cocktail parties (two sherries, one Perrier, for rational results). If you can manage a drink with the group's executive, you can do an unobtrusive dry run (wet or medium-dry run?) of your main speech themes, watching like a slightly absentminded hawk for reactions.

You can also do well by playing dumb (which is often easy if you're a contractor talking to poets, or vice versa). Just ask innocently "What are the main things you guys are worried about for the next year, and what would you like to see done?" They'll love you for asking, and when your tactfully brief cocktail stay is over, you will have spotted the two or three hopes and fears which will allow you to zero in miraculously on your audience's real concerns.

I say "real" concerns, because often your assigned topic will prove outdated, too vague, or incomplete. If you find that your "prepared improvisation" seems precisely in harmony with your hosts' wishes, then stick with it, and have another sherry. If, as is usual, you find you could usefully update or enrich your talk—or even just steal some current in-joke or obsession that will bring you closer to your newfound friends—return to your room, glance at your notes, and make a change or two.

In the rare case that you find your prepared talk is wildly out of your audience's orbit, don't be afraid to change your basic plan. Very often this only demands reshuffling sections or taking another theme for your unifying allegory.

If, for example, you have a plan with sound structural logic but unsuitable metaphors, you simply rebaptize your introductory theme and your section headings. Let's say you have a three-part allegory on raising children as a builder raises a house (good design and good cement make good character). Then you find out that your audience cares more for classical music than for houses. So you switch allegories to tell them that raising kids is like Beethoven's growth as a composer (rigorous early discipline, plus measured experiments with freedom, lead to movingly controlled power).

If such cosmetic repairs won't do the trick, you must go back to square one. Retire early, and rethink a better core-theme and structure under the vivifying terror of your shrinking deadline. Believe me, you will produce. Better yet, because you now *know* it's on target, what you produce will restore the confidence that just crumbled when you learned you were off the track.

The second way to get into your audience's skin supposes you don't have this eve-of-speech lead time. You must do this less probing, but still refreshing, plug-in during the half hour or so preceding your speech.

Again you excuse yourself from your solicitous hosts. If they cling too much, make a pained glance toward the washroom, disappear, then climb out the washroom window—or whatever exit you need to take to get away from idle protocol.

Free at last, you latch onto two or three unofficial-looking delegates and take your "crowd bath" with as much sensitive, casual grace as you can muster. Since few of your unsuspecting button-hole preys will know yet who you are, you can probably massage their minds and hearts with a minimum of self-conscious fuss.

Never, of course, be underhanded. If the moment or topic seems apt, you should identify yourself. But keep it simple and unstuffy. Who do you think you are, anyway?

As you can sense by now, the aim of all this nudging and snuggling is simply to put you further at ease. At least half of your natural fear about speaking is fear of not knowing your audience. Just as unvoiced hugging of wife and kids can keep you close to them, these subtle little pre-platform squeezings will maneuver you and your public into the first tender steps of your tango. Audiences have personalities. To frolic nimbly and cozily, get acquainted before you go out on the dance floor.

If, in spite of all your tries at pre-platform intimacy, you face the footlights in an uncontrollable fit of trembling, use this old standby favored by Merv Griffin and Jerry Lewis: when butterflies attack, step close to your audience. If the microphone is set high on the stage, you cannot readily do this, short of shaking a hand or two on your way up. If it is on a level with your listeners, though, move it forward so that you feel enveloped and protected by that hardy first row.

Only nice people, I've found, sit in the first row. They are either journalists eager to quote you or enthusiasts who, in advance, have judged you to be a smash hit.

Pretend that all your enemies are sitting in the last row. Speak first to your "friends" up front—then work your way back!

2. Psych Up, Offstage and On

All great stage performers, from Artur Rubinstein to Liberace, from Charles de Gaulle to Rich Little, taught themselves early in the game how to quell the unholy stirrings of panic. Every artist, including you, must work out by trial and error an arsenal of tummy soothers: munching cookies, doing chin-ups on the curtain rods, counting to two hundred in Tibetan—anything that works.

Let's call a speech a speech. What you need to do at this point is to kid yourself—or rather to fool your jumpy nerves. You need to divert your surging energy away from your innards, which it will tear apart, and toward your audience, with whom you hope to draw together.

A silly game? Self-delusion? Precisely. Call it charlatanism for the soul. As you step to the podium, are you agonizing in self-doubt and self-consciousness? To save you from destructive narcissism, we've got to turn your attention from you to your listeners.

How to rechannel your emotions? First prepare your body and mind to let energy flow outward. Then convince yourself that you are swamping your audience with cascades of your Niagara-like power. Move from narcissism to mild megalomania. Do not guffaw. At this pre-stage stage, you really feel as though you are *going over* Niagara Falls in a barrel.

The first step, getting your energy to flow outward, calls for some blend of body-over-mind exercises that work for you. Your stage fright is largely psychosomatic, and you must cure it by reversing the process of mind bugging body. Calisthenics, walking, jogging, or anything that expands your cardiovascular activity is helpful. If you know a spot of yoga or meditation, do that as briefly as you need.

For ending off your regimen, or even replacing it completely if time is cut to seconds or a very few minutes, try deep breathing. The very last thing you should be doing before taking any floor, indeed, should be to steal three or four deep-from-the-belly inhalations. Your mind can be rehearsing your opening lines. But your tummy should be rising and falling like Mount St. Helen's in slow motion.

Deep breathing helps you in two ways. First, it almost instantly calms your nerves—reducing hysteria to something like controlled nightmares. Second, it drops your voice about an octave. When you hear your voice at a tense, tight high C, that alone will speed your panic. When deep breathing drops you down to a fair imitation of a *basso profundo,* your booming, authoritative tones will persuade you that a person with such a well-modulated voice knows the score. Try a bit of belly-breathing; you'll impress yourself.

Maybe most women would rather not sound like Paul Robeson. Don't worry—you'll come off as a nice throaty contralto. Say, if you smoke a lot, like Cleo Laine.

Whatever pitch you find, this deep breathing will put you in fine spirits for your second step: playing your secret little domination farce with your audience. By this time, we assume you've got the nerves stilled and the juices flowing outward, with body leading mind. Now we consolidate your conquest of yourself by training your mind to confirm that you are about to conquer your audience.

This bit of fun is simple, and allows you to enjoy all the ecstasies of Don Rickles. It's insult time—time to mouth or murmur to yourself, just at the last second before you go on, exactly what a person of your extraordinary talents—thinks of the peons below.

The lesson lies in a charming device which the legendary classical singer Emmy Heim used to resort to when she was bowing to acknowledge the applause before she sang. She would bow deeply and humbly, smiling like an angel, then nod sweetly left, right, and center to her audience while whispering to herself: "To hell with you, to hell with you, and to hell with you."

The audience probably thought she was saying "How kind of you." If you can stand a small giggle to crack the last-second tension, make up your own little saying to remind you that your audience is not a firing squad. Just stick to the general spirit of Emmy Heim or, if you prefer, Clark Gable's "Frankly, my dear, I don't give a damn."

3. Listen to Who You Are

This piece of counsel does not flatter your narcissism; it only reminds you that courtesy and common sense are Siamese twins.

How many speeches have you sat through (not enjoyed) where the host introduced the speaker with elaborate detail and grace, then the speaker ignored the introduction and plunged in with his own precooked masterpiece? Such behavior is not just rude; it is stupid and self-denying. On one hand, it brands the speaker as a clod suffering either from a big-star complex or the amateur's fear of getting sidetracked from a rigidly written text. On the other, it prevents the speaker from savoring, and profiting from, an often elegant and ice-breaking beginning.

You would be surprised at how many so-called big-time speakers in the political and business world come to the stage armed not only with the full text of their speech itself, but with every laborious, insincere word acknowledging their introduction written out as well. Stuff like: "Thank you, Mr. Chairman. Your words were moving and all too flattering [I'll say they were]. Let me begin by saying how happy I am to be among you on this important occasion in your fine city. I am also glad that so many of your charming wives were able to join us."

Ugh. You will have recognized nearly every cliché, banality, and web-footed putdown in the repertoire. Yet, believe me, there are legions of louts who peddle such claptrap. They cannot even see the hilarity in their failure to recognize that, by definition, all speakers are happy to be where they are, all the hosts' occasions are important, all home cities are fine, and all wives (even when they are Margaret Thatcher, with husband at home) are charming.

A good speaker will proclaim his quality by his very first words. Even though the first words of the *conceptual* part of your speech must also sound a trumpet or two, you should learn—indeed force yourself by real risk to learn—how to exploit each introduction. This practice will take many times to get to a finely honed skill, but even if you fail a few times, you can work up to an honorable and ornamental standard by trying.

The key is *listening*. You must finish your last-minute mental run-throughs of your plan *before* the introduction. For the few seconds or minutes during which your host explains and praises you and your topic, you must tune in to *his* words, not yours.

Ideally, you should try to spot some word, image, or joke of his that can lead you pleasingly into your topic. If you see no such opening, you should at least tune in—to what he says to see if you can pick up on his thoughts.

If you can do so, you will mark yourself, from the very outset of your performance, as a confident, experienced, courteous person. And if you are all that, you don't need the hackneyed toadyism that so often passes for polished ritual among the pompous and insecure.

Should you manage to pull off a truly and obviously improvised lead-in repartee, your task of seducing the audience will have already made a giant step. You will have earned a sympathy that you might have needed half an hour to build through the jump-in-cold technique. And your ego—a key to eloquence—will swell hearteningly.

Lovely, but how? Well, we presume that with all the huffing and puffing and deep-breathing you've already done, you've simmered down to a low boil. You have listened to your gushing presenter with a convincing blush and attentive ears. Now, the mood of your reply must vary —with the spirit of the occasion and the host's own tone. Let's look at some typical situations.

Most times, if you are facing a large, fresh audience, you will be lucky enough to hear your host lay on the compliments with a trowel. This may wound your modesty, but you will no doubt manage to survive the bouquets' perfume with only passing dizziness.

Let's say your host at the convention of the Amalgamated Weed-Pickers Union portrays you as the most *honest* man (I'll underline exploitable words, then your pick-up) ever to *stir up* the public authorities on the vital matter of weeds. Given that weeds, however annoying, are not usually a tragic topic, you can afford a little innocent punning to convey your sublime humility: "Ladies and gentlemen, I don't know if I'm the most honest man ever to put a *burr under the government's saddle* on weeds; for such a good cause, I've often been tempted to do some 'dandy lyin'.'" On second thought, if you can't do better than that, lay off puns.

If, to change the mood, you are winging a eulogy at your business rival's funeral, you might hear a brief but unctuous intro such as: "And now, to emphasize how deeply Herbert Rippemoff will be missed even outside his firm, we are honored to welcome his most *distinguished* competitor, Mr. Adam Smith, who has *journeyed* to join us from across the continent." To which, rolling eyes heavenward as you count how Herb's departure will spur your own sales, you intone: "Friends and relatives of Herb, we are *all distinguished* today, distinguished by the privilege of having loved this remarkable man called Herbert Rippemoff. It is *his journey*, not yours or mine, which we wish to ponder today—and, I believe, learn from." You can't always have such fun: pathos with profits.

Another typical scene might place you in front of an office meeting where everybody knows you, or where your biography is not needed. The chairman, say, is just asking round-robin opinions, and turns to you for your five- or ten-minute spiel. He might still hand you a usable pick-up phrase: "Our next view on microprocessors comes from Alicia Orangeblossom of our printing department which, as you know, is responsible for our *beautifully* produced *annual reports.*

You, Alicia, do a self-mocking, endearing little pick-up such as: "Mr. Chairman, not to oversell our services, I assure you that the printing department is responsible for putting *beauty* only in the annual report's physical appearance; credit for this year's *beautiful bottom line* must go to Financial Services . . . (an oily pause) . . . and I trust that this well-timed compliment will move our Financial friends to give our department the *beautiful* new printing press we've been lobbying for." Flattery, plus a dash of cynicism, will get you everywhere.

Sometimes you find yourself on hostile terrain, as a known enemy of your audience. This time your host may give you a brusque, if not quite coarse, build-up. Your best weapons: courtesy and humor. For example, you, a partisan of abortion on demand, are invited (fat chance!) to speak to a group of right-to-lifers. Like pro- and anti-nuclear people, "pro-choice" and "pro-life" factions never talk with each other, only past each other. But let's imagine a miracle has been, er, born, and you are on before the save-the-fetus folk. Your host presents you as "a *well-meaning murderer*, a *misguided* dismantler of society who spouts slogans of freedom while following the eugenic doctrines of the *Nazis*."

A gentle lead-in, so to speak.

Your host tried to give you the benefit of the doubt by calling you well-meaning and misguided, but he overplayed his hand with the hyperbolic "murderer" and "Nazis." You must fling both condescending compliments and slander back in his teeth—all the while smiling respectfully as befits Daniel in the lions' den: "I am grateful to be excused as only a *well-meaning* murderer. It's consoling also to know that I dismantle society only because I'm *misguided*. But I'm perplexed at being linked to the Nazis. As I recall, the Nazis were, like some others today, opposed to freedom of choice."

A low polemic, not at all the thing for tea parties.

Another stumper for the stump speaker is the in-a-way-encouraging but hard-to-live-up-to lead-in: "Our next speaker needs no introduction, so here she is, Gloria S. Transit." Gloria, in *flagrante delicto* of deep breathing, had better recover fast, or her fame *will* prove fleeting. Perhaps she could try, if the occasion is not too solemn, something

like: "When somebody tells me I don't need any introduction, I always wonder if it's because they couldn't find
anything nice to say. . . ."

Occasionally your host will find all too much that is
nice to say. You may have supplied a curriculum vitae in
the form of a smorgasbord—a detailed, all-purpose one
meant to be picked at, not devoured. Alas, some literal-
minded hosts believe they must tell all, which is more than
either you or your audience really cares to hear about you.

Risking only your reputation as a self-advertising twit
who circulates your life story to people who barely wanted
to know how to spell your name, you must endure the in-
terminable list of your schools, accomplishments, awards,
and family data. Then you can deflate it all with some
mock-serious protest: "It was kind of Dr. Guillotine to list
my six doctorates, my Nobel Prize in chemistry, and my
circumnavigation of the globe in a canoe. But I'm sorry he
did not have time to mention that, at age eleven, I won the
igloo-building contest in Moose Jaw, Saskatchewan."

A variation on this trial-by-excess is the elaborately
cute introduction. Once I squirmed through a five-minute
intro using each letter of my name as a trampoline for a
maudlin little essay on my virtues (I have only eleven of
them, one for each letter of K-E-I-T-H S-P-I-C-E-R).
K, claimed my kill-'em-with-kindness tormentor, stood for
knowledge—or was it knavery or kleptomania? Whatever
it was, it went on and on and on. By the time I got to the
mike, those still left in the audience were sick of hearing
about me, and hostile to hearing from me on any subject at
all. The best diversion I could come up with to shift the
glare from me to my too-eager host was: "By now I'm sure

you'd all like to hear what he could do by spelling out my vices."

That barely got the show back on the road. I just wish I had thought of this far snappier line which a more quick-witted female colleague whispered that I should have said: "Just be glad my name is not Nikolai Rimsky-Korsakov."

Inspired. Pointed, yet not cruel. If your audience had dug night baseball more than *The Thousand and One Nights of Scheherazade,* I suppose Cornelius McGillicuddy would have served as well.

4. Listen to Your Voice

Just a short tip for the first thirty seconds of your talk: listen dispassionately to your voice's pitch and modulation. Get them right from the outset. "Right" means deep, relaxed, controlled.

A couple of pages back we cited the merits of deep breathing in dropping your normal stage screech to a nice, warm belly-tone. In spite of your most valiant efforts to speak from the tummy as well as the heart, you may find that last-second mike fright has turned you back into Tweetie the Canary. Resolve, as you open your mouth, to cut in clearly and firmly at high decibels but low frequency. Stretch your ears for the first few sentences until you manage to master a voice that you like and believe.

To make it sound relaxed, you are wise to deliberately speak more slowly than usual. It's easy, and natural, to speed up as enthusiasm and the power of your own splendid arguments carry you forward. Slowing down sounds less elegant: listeners suspect either that you are losing steam or that you are struggling to calm your nerves.

The illusion of control is no illusion. It comes from authoritative pitch, stately pace, and careful diction. If you tend normally to mumble, mangle, and massacre your words, don't. Retrain yourself to enunciate something closely resembling English. Remember Demosthenes, the greatest of the Greeks in tongue: he practiced with pebbles in his mouth. When he spoke publicly without pebbles, his diction tripped out crisp and clear—or so he muttered.

If, on stage, you sound more like Demosthenes rehearsing than performing, slow down and try to chisel out each word. Don't enunciate so cuttingly that you sound like a record of "How now, brown cow?" or "The rain in Spain lies mainly in the plain," but distinctly enough so that nobody can nickname you Marble-mouth.

Do all this, and you will charm yourself—the vital prelude to charming your audience. Remember that the charming voice you seek must be a true one which, however disciplined, faithfully echoes your personality. A stagy, phony voice does not charm. It jars.

5. Look at Your Audience

During all this personal psychotherapy, have you been betraying your lingering terror by glancing alternately at your shoes and the ceiling? Remember this: you are looking high and low for your audience, and it is not there.

Your listeners camp in front of you, sometimes around you. To carry off your rhetorical seduction, you must use

the means of communication which the Prophet Mo-
hammed rightly warned led to all wooing—the eyes.
Straight-on, frank, probing eye-contact.

We talked earlier of scanning audiences, of crisscross-
ing to seek feedback, to record reactions. Now—again in
the first few seconds or minutes of your talk—you must
scan your audience with a calm, systematic eye. Before
looking for the reactions you may seek later on as signals
to shift or hold your ground, you need your audience's eyes
for two very practical needs.

The first lies in the dynamics of the *winging it* method
itself. You will recall that, while speaking, you imagine an
invisible teleprompter rolling your speech outline or plan
past your eyes. This requires a fairly stable "screen" in
your mind, and this you can best maintain by holding your
audience in a pretty steady gaze. Such a gaze is also the
best way to *seduce your audience*. If you jump your eyes
back and forth between floor and chandeliers, you may
lose both your way and your charisma.

No doubt you could easily track your plan by staring at
the floor—but who wants to seduce a floor? The "action" is
straight ahead of you, and you must never forget that all
your actions—plan, voice, gestures, appearance—must
contrive to rally the folks in front of you.

The second need to satisfy in keeping a close, frank
eye on your audience has to do with building a constituency. Before you start speaking, and in the first minutes
after you begin, you must feed your confidence and momentum by locating sympathetic faces.

If you have already done a fair bit of speaking, you will
know how many different types of faces you encounter in

an audience when you start "cold": some skeptical, others bored, some hostile, some ready to doze off, a precious few eager to hear you. Latch on to those happy few (most of them, as we said, being at or near the front), lock eyes with each one in turn—and forget the rest.

These eager beavers will nourish you and encourage you enough for twenty indifferent listeners. Begin your long, slow seduction with those who want to be seduced. Interest yourself in the others only gradually as you sense your magic working across the crowd. When the insensitive mob realize that you are making oratorical love with their neighbors, they will catch on that you are a charmer. They will begin vying for your eyes like neglected spaniels.

Confronted no more by ugly-tempered human beings but by cuddly beavers and spaniels, how can you possibly stay nervous?

6. Roll the Credits

And now, your secret weapon: the mind's-eye teleprompter. During your rehearsals and warm-ups—which might have lasted five minutes or three hours—you practiced visualizing your plan, then running it slowly past your eyes. At first, you may have sharpened the image of your point-form script by closing your eyes. Then you ran it through with eyes open to make sure it did not fade before an audience.

If you have taken the time your existing memory skills demand, you will catch on to all this, and you will get better and better. After you have spent a few days or weeks drilling yourself in three-part plans in the ways described in Chapter Six, you will progress quickly. The magic of "projecting" the invisible teleprompter inside your head will become second nature.

Do not despair if your imaginary screen goes blank from time to time. It happens to all of us sometimes, even to the best. Remember what Horace said of flagging genius: "But if Homer, usually good, nods for a moment, I think it shame." Shame, but so natural, so forgivable. If ancient Homer could keep his reputation in spite of an occasional blank-out, you should not freeze and give up if once in a while you blow it—especially while apprenticing.

In the next chapter, we'll discuss bailout procedures if, even as an accomplished performer, your memory-motor conks out and sends you into a tailspin.

Right now, we just want to get you started. Assuming you really have drilled yourself enough in your plan's outline, you should start your talk by concentrating on three teleprompter dimensions: lighting, focus, and speed.

If you have ever used a teleprompter, you will know that one of your worst enemies in scanning the little square screen is shadows. You have spotlights in your eyes, others hitting the camera lens over which the teleprompter mirror sits, and all manner of fluky reflections and refractions. Unless you get your lighting right before the camera flicks on, you may end up reading "bunk" for "bank" or "golf" for "gulf." If you do decipher the moving text through all the glints and fade-outs, you may end up squinting like Grandma Moses painting a grasshopper.

In a real-life studio, you must fiddle with the studio and teleprompter lights until you can see every corner of the tiny screen easily. The same goes for the make-believe screen in your head. Just as you "order" the screen to turn up the first title-line of your talk, make an effort of will to force the whole screen to come alive, bright and clear, with razor-sharp contrast. Pretend you are turning on high-wattage lights to enhance your message—and—thanks to this hokey bit of self-delusion—it will shine.

By focus I mean you should let your imagination call forth only one line at a time. Once you see your text plainly, don't try to project the whole thing before your eyes at once. If you do, it will scare you. Indeed, in a blur of words which are masses of letters instead of clear ideas, your screen will confuse you, not save and guide you.

Again, in real-life teleprompter work, you should try to read only the line which is rolling up past the *center* of the camera lens. The rest you ignore. What has already rolled upward you don't need anymore; what's coming along you should not mix up with what you already are reading. If you do, you will lose the eye-expressions and voice-inflections that indicate you genuinely understand your words. These convince your audience that you are not reading at all, but improvising with uncommon eloquence.

Finally, you should complete your start-of-speech tune-up by getting your speed right. You must command your mind's-eye teleprompter to move upward only at a pace that suits you. Suiting you means following your thoughts, not crowding them. It means relaxing you, not tensing you. It means sustaining and nourishing your ideas, giving you confidence and, if need be, rescuing you.

All of this, as you realize by now, is one big con game on yourself. By fooling yourself into these disciplines of imagination, you will learn to create a happy illusion of improvisation for your audience. As long as you are telling your own truths as you see them, and as long as you are not scanning a real teleprompter or sneaking a peek at notes on your cuffs, such phantom-games are fair ball, even good fun.

I would counsel, as you've seen, only one fail-safe cheater's trick: carry your one-page summary plan with you in a pocket onstage. Just knowing it's there is your insurance against ever needing it.

The real secret of success in winging it lies in never taking any of these tricks too seriously. If you become solemn and literal about the gentle trickery traced out here, your somberness will tinge the flavor of your whole speech. You don't want to come off as a pompous ass, do you?

If you do, then—forgive me—maybe you are one. Just don't forget—that if you insist on being pompous you had better be extraordinarily good. I'm sure you are. But why let pretentious nonsense lose you listeners? Count every speech as an election campaign, and nail down every vote you can cajole, browbeat, or preferably seduce to your side.

I don't know if you can seduce anybody while fastening your seat belt, but as you solo off to the oratorical skies, I think you'd better try. Our only trifling problem now is to keep you aloft, and that's what we'll seek to do in the next chapter.

Bon voyage, Lindbergh. Paris is closer than you think.

Speak the speech, I pray you, as I pronounced it to you, trippingly on the tongue; but if you mouth it, as many of your players do, I had as lief the town-crier spoke my lines. Nor do not saw the air too much with your hand, thus; but use all gently: for in the very torrent, tempest, and—as I may say—whirlwind of passion, you must acquire and beget a temperance, that may give it smoothness.

—SHAKESPEARE, *Hamlet*

CHAPTER NINE

Twelve Ways Not To Crash

At last we've got you airborne. To win your pilot's license for hot-air flying, all you need is to memorize the following little handbook on oratorical aerodynamics. The rules below aim 1) to bring your message and personality clearly and sympathetically to your listeners, and 2) to keep you cool in the cockpit, confident and serene as you soar—not over their heads but into their minds. We'll begin with basics, then work through some refinements—such as landing when you run out of gas.

1. Underline Your Plan

Sticking to our allegory of flying, think of this as your flight plan. It really is. It pinpoints your destination, traces your itinerary, even guides you on weather—here the atmospherics of the audience's background and mood.

The bedrock idea in using your plan to best effect is the one you apply to squeezing the most joy out of a good meal or any two of your ten other favorite activities: talk about it before, during, and after. As we said above, the reasons for repeating your plan out loud three times are to impress your ideas and approach on your audience, and to help you recall where you are on your invisible map: your "Cartesian teleprompter."

To begin, in the first few sentences of your introduction (right after you state your topic), you should sketch out the three or four steps of your plan. Then, as you arrive at each main part or sub-part, you should fleetingly restate the heading you are going to deal with. As you sum up at the very end, you should wrap up your trip by quickly recalling—often in one sentence—how leading your listeners through the three or four stages has brought them to your conclusion.

To summarize: Announce your plan; follow your plan; and recapitulate your plan. This is not far different from what a good teacher or a paternalistic politician would advise, quite apart from plans, just to get ideas into an audience's heads: tell them first what you're going to tell them, tell them next what you're telling them, and finally remind them of what you've just told them.

Why such harping on structure again? Because you are doing television without a screen. You are teaching without a blackboard. If your listeners are not to get lost, you need to replace *visual* underlining by *verbal* underlining.

Such emphasis and repetition bring you and your listeners together in several ways. The main payoff lies in helping your audience "read" your outline with you. Stating your plan clearly at the outset, then gracefully highlighting its headings as you move along enables hearers to "see" ideas as well as hear words. It situates them in a soon-familiar framework which reassures, guides, and clarifies. In this way, it allows an audience to follow you closely, even on a complex or technical topic. Whenever the going gets a bit rough, the technicalities a bit heavy, you draw your listeners back to the neon-bright flight path you pointed to at the beginning.

A second advantage emerges in the way your restated and followed outline Mau-Maus your audience. The whole sequence of announcing a plan, then picking it up at specified intervals eloquently stresses your logic, coherence, discipline, and mastery of the topic. You'll find that most audiences fall into mild awe just because they witness you speaking for some time without notes. When you add to the ability to fly solo the skill of being able to navigate precisely a long trip without any maps in sight, you will subjugate even the toughest, most skeptical audience. This does not mean you can get away with any kind of nonsense; but this aura of mental rigor puts you psychologically one up on your audience. It predisposes most people to think that, even though your ideas are crazy, you are not a dunce. In times of adversity for your particular cause, a reputation for not being stupid will console you poignantly.

A final benefit comes in the insidious way your reminders of part headings, and your repetitive "1, 2, and 3" approach, keep your audience alert. They can jolt awake some folks who are inclined to doze. Most flattering of all, they tend to encourage a few eager beavers to take notes. You make it all sound so simple, clear, and logical that they just can't resist recording your wisdom. Think of the thrill to your quavering ego: while you wing your way through the terrors of your invisible outline, some people believe your words are bright enough to preserve—if not for posterity, at least until they leave the hall.

One crucial caveat: beware of restating your outline too obviously. The essence of art is artless disguise. You must stick relentlessly to your plan, even trying to stay close to certain code words in the headings you announced in your intro. But if you do this too clumsily, too mechanically, you will sound like a puppet. You will sound like—Heaven forbid—someone who bought a book on rhetoric and, overcome with insecurity, rote-learned its lessons.

If elegance strains your mind or theme, try simplicity, as did Cicero in this unflashy transition in his speech *On the Command of Cnaeus Pompeius:* "Now that I have said something about the character of the war, it remains for me to add a few words about its dimensions."

Follow this rule of "underlining" your plan carefully, but not slavishly. Don't say dumb, flat-footed things like "And now, for my second part, entitled 'The nesting habits of Brazilian lizards.'" Be suave, be smooth. Let it flow naturally. Say, for example: "Now you know how Brazilian lizards eat. Would you like to know where they sleep?"

Probably there's nothing your audience would more passionately care to know.

As for beginnings and endings, use the same informal formality. Wrap up your rigid plan in the easy flow of normal speech. You may, and often should, resort to numbers ("first, second, and third"), but don't make it all sound like a parrot reciting a math book. The sign of the accomplished speaker, as of any polished artist, is to hide his art without hiding his point. Strive for clarity with subtlety.

If there is any time you can sin in the direction of clarity instead of subtlety, it's when you first announce your plan. If you don't imprint your plan indelibly on your listeners' minds then, they may not know what to try to follow during your speech. At the start, after defining your topic ("The sensual life of Brazilian lizards"), state your plan slowly and deliberately. Do so as if to telegraph your flight plan to a bunch of air traffic controllers who you fear may be half asleep.

State baldly: "We're going to look first at how Brazilian lizards eat; next at how they nest; and finally, if you don't mind a little X-rated zoology, at what they do in those nests to make more Brazilian lizards."

Whether or not your audience is asleep by the time you reach your ending, you should round off things by a quick, satisfying recap of your plan, leaning more to subtlety. If you hammer home too brutally, too numerically, the inexorable progress you have made through the listeners' earlier fog, you may leave a last impression best called schoolmasterish.

Your recap need touch only lightly on your logic's way-stations. It should do so with a flourish—bearing in mind that the folks will soon be filing out to mutter how brilliant or tedious you were. A small flash of poetry, of wit, of irony, often serves.

Let's try: "And so the whole life of our friend the Brazilian lizard adds up to nothing more than eating, nesting, and procreating. I ask you this: If lizards are so low on the scale of reincarnation, how come they, unlike us, only have fun?" No doubt Jacques Cousteau could find a deeper significance.

Practice mixing clarity and subtlety on graver topics than lizards. You will find that the basic rule about art disguising discipline remains. Think of it as seeking artistic unity—cohesion of structure, content, and taste. Not *rigor mortis* but *rigor artis*.

2. Keep It Simple

"Nobody ever went broke," growled H. L. Mencken, "underestimating the intelligence of the American public." The media's intellectual poverty in other lands doesn't always lead to bankruptcy either. But don't be a snob. Before elegance, cleverness, color, wit, and every other virtue stands clarity. And clarity is almost synonymous with simplicity. If you are not simple and direct in your speech, there's a good chance you don't know what you want to say. As poet Nicolas Boileau told the court of Louis XIV: "Well-shaped ideas always speak clearly, and the words to phrase them never cost dearly."

Now that we're mucking about at Versailles, you could do worse than remember the rehearsal technique used by our old pal the Sun King's master preacher, Bossuet. A specialist in trembly tear-jerkers for royal funerals, Bossuet tested his orations for clarity by declaiming them to his maid. If she could understand what he was saying, reasoned the cunning cleric, so could a duke or a marquise.

The ploy still works. If you tend to be wordy, just ask your spouse to play Bossuet's maid. Do a dry run with him or her to see if you can explain your subject in plain English. Your spouse, if you tell him or her the courtly precedent, will no doubt be hugely flattered. If your spouse and/or lover takes offense, a child of medium brainpower will do as well.

As a matter of fact, I've found a good way to force myself to think clearly is to imagine explaining my subject to a twelve-year-old child. Not because I think twelve-year-olds are slow, but because they are demanding. I prefer children as guinea pigs because they are "simpleminded" in the sense of insisting, more than most bafflegab-tolerant adults, that people explain themselves intelligibly. If you are not clear with children, they will drive you insane—or rather sane—with questions.

I also like kids for dry runs or as an imaginary audience because they criticize your opinions more frankly. Perhaps best of all, they can see through phoniness like a laser cutting butter.

I don't advise going as far as G.O.P. congressman Guy

Vander Jagt, the man who gave the keynote speech at the 1980 Republican convention. He rehearsed by declaiming to the squirrels and pine trees near his Michigan home. I've never met a squirrel I didn't like, but I have some doubts about the critical faculties of pine trees.

3. Follow Fowler, etc.

This book does not aim to teach you to write. But you will speak far more clearly if you absorb a few rules honored by the best writers.

Although bookshelves groan under archives of handbooks on style, the most succinct listing of tricks graces the classic work by the long-dead Fowler brothers from England. The Fowlers lead off their book, *The King's English*, with the commanding and commendable statement that, before seeking "the more showy qualities," a good writer should strive to be "direct, simple, brief, vigorous, and lucid."

To be all this, they advise that you recall the following five rules. I have found them, along with a couple more which I'll throw in for the same price, a fine set of guidelines for reaching what I think is the goal of all easy-to-register writing and speaking: putting pictures in people's heads. Here are the Fowler rules, with my examples in parentheses:

1. *Prefer the familiar word to the farfetched* (forefather instead of progenitor).

2. *Prefer the concrete word to the abstract* (knife instead of cutlery). Think of this also as preferring the specific to the general.

3. *Prefer the single word to the circumlocution.* ("He was vague" instead of—such horrors happen all the time—"the specificity of his intentions did not immediately demonstrate itself.")

4. *Prefer the short word to the long* ("bank" instead of "banking institution").

5. *Prefer the Saxon word to the Romance.* If you studied Latin in high school, you'll know the difference. If not, you might try guessing that Saxon words are the ones that seem to fit whiskey-drinkers, and Latin words the ones that fit wine-drinkers ("cold" instead of "frigid"—or should we say, in homage to both, "well chilled").

The Fowler brothers summed up all five of their rules in the following blockbuster bombast: "in the contemplated eventuality" is farfetched, abstract, roundabout, long, and Latin-rooted. All it means is the plain English "if so."

Think over these pointers sometime you really want to clean up your English act. Then add these two rules from the journalist's trade: use active verbs instead of passive ones, and chop out as many adjectives and adverbs as you can without making your talk or writing sound like a garbled telegram. Active verbs ("He hit the ball" instead of "the ball was hit by him") put juice and drive in your sentences. Cutting out qualifiers cures clutter.

If you try tidying up your written English with these well-accepted tricks, you'll find your writing correcting your speech.

This discipline, even though you must practice it over months and years, will guide you more and more unconsciously when you are on your feet. Obviously, you cannot keep scanning these rules all the way through each speech; if you did, you would not have time to remember what you wanted to say. But make a long-term effort to infect your talk with these standard guidelines of sound English.

Even if your ideas start to wear thin, your style—lean, clean, and zingy—will become as "listenable" as Perry Como's. *It's Impossible?* Not at all.

4. Nail Down Each Point

All these hints attempt to help you become light of foot while solid on your feet. But you must take care not to glide so lightly over your material that you blur your topic into fine-sounding incoherence. You must distinguish your points. To make sense, to forge logic, you must mark off each argument in its turn, giving it play enough, and depth and color enough, to strike home. Here's a useful little ploy. Think of each point in three phases (again? again): state, illustrate, comment. In other words, tell what, how, and why.

Let's try an example or two. You are a drug manufacturer explaining to a group of pharmacists a dazzling new amphetamine which flies you to the moon for thirty minutes, then drops you tenderly in a parachute to these surly bonds of earth: the perfect recipe for becoming an instant manic-depressive.

First you explain what your wonder pill does, and chuckle as you spell out its suspenseful acronym (WGU— What Goes Up . . .). Next you tell whom it will help— let's say the busy executive who needs a substitute for a coffee break to avoid cancer of the pancreas. Finally, you assess the significance of your Ping-Pong pill for career-minded executives in a snappy, memorable phrase or formula: "Get a raise by getting a rise." Say no more of the upwardly mobile.

Another example might cast you as the manager of a major commercial bank downtown. You are, of course, a woman. Your task? To explain to your mortgage staff a mouth-watering new policy headquarters has just approved. First you sum up the new mortgage terms (a 4 percent reduction for unwed mothers and struggling writers). Next you weave a little anecdote about how such a bonus will allow many more women to start families without the encumbrance of a man. Finally, you describe this plan as the biggest breakthrough in women's lib since the vacuum cleaner (ahem).

As for writers? Your new mortgages, by making lazy scribblers into real-estate speculators, should leave only one in ten writers still writing, thereby improving the quality of literature overnight. No "next books" as collateral, please—but we'll look at clients who keep their points punchy.

One taken-for-granted way to nail down points is to "illustrate" your talk with images, symbols, and vocabulary that your audience identifies with. If you are addressing civil engineers, don't exemplify the value of disciplined innovation by informing them that Beethoven used trombones for the first time only in his Fifth Symphony. You might try a reference, if you must be classy, to the use of keystones in early Roman viaducts. Better still, stay simple, straight, and yourself (presuming you are not an engineer), and tell them how your father would not let you have Meccano set No. 4 until you had mastered all the tricks of set No. 3.

In many cases, you will be an expert talking to experts in the same field: a school superintendent speaking to teachers, a sales manager for GM talking to car salesmen, a second-story man lecturing to safecrackers. On these in-house occasions, your examples pose no problem—except the mighty one of imagination.

When you are off your home turf—say, as an accountant advising dentists of the latest juicy tax dodge—you really should try to borrow some imagery from your listeners' own interests. It's more than mere courtesy; it's a smart way to evoke sympathy. It's a case of impact, relevance, efficiency—call it just getting heard. (On second thought, allusions to drilling holes in the tax laws to put gold fillings in Swiss banks might be carrying "audience aptness" a bit far.)

5. Let Emotions
Follow Thoughts

A lovely fringe benefit of winging it is that by hanging tough for improvisation you will learn to hang loose.

So far we've spoken a lot about how flying by a remembered outline frees your mind. It also unchains your emotions to a degree impossible when you read a text.

In this era of touchy-feely letting go, such a boon is timely. It should become a normal dimension of any speech at any time or place. I'm not pleading that you should wring your heart dry on a survey of accounting procedures for car parts or of cataloguing systems for species of snails. I'm arguing that you should relax and enjoy the flow of genuine enthusiasm, sadness, ecstasy, or whatever else your subject moves you to feel.

Such honest emotion does two things for your speech. It strengthens the impression of sincerity and authenticity you need to convey to be credible. And it can stimulate your imagination to a natural eloquence.

What we're talking about is our old ploy of rechanneling terror—the device of changing the negative tension of fear into the positive drive of inspiration. It's a matter of psyching yourself up to believe that your tummy holds a reservoir of creative energy instead of a snakepit of anxiety.

This is a powerful concept for those who really wilt under stage fright. We need not belabor the point further than saying that you should believe this works and practice it. Soon you will sense the joy of peeling the layers of fright off that ball in your stomach. Beneath them all you will discover a fuel cell to power your thoughts into pulses your audience cannot ignore.

Be careful, though. It will not do if you writhe onstage in laughter at your own jokes, or begin blubbering as you recount some tragic tale. What you are after here is the most exciting spectacle of all: contained emotion, feelings reined in by an act of will. From your own snakepit you will emerge as a coiled python—grace, menace, imminent surprise. Eyes will be riveted on you. Your gripping words will be punctuated only by the clangor of dropped pins.

6. Use Humor Naturally

Or do we mean "naturally, use humor"? Whichever way, unless the occasion is unalterably sad, you can reinforce your points, highlight transitions, or pace your rhythm with apt excursions into wit. Apart from these more formal functions, humor allows you two psychological advantages.

On one hand, it breaks the tension of an otherwise dry or heavy topic. It keeps the audience on board when fatigue or overload tempts them to abandon your ship to daydream. You know this effect. It's the "sugaring-the-pill" strategy: using a legitimate irony or oddity to illuminate a hard-to-swallow truth. Example: after droning on for five minutes about the spiritual joys of collecting and mounting rare stamps, you could toss in a little throwaway line like "if you don't crave poetic satisfactions, remember that you can sell these sticky little scraps of paper for outrageous profits!"

On the other hand, humor—particularly gentle irony or wild hyperbole—can let you make your points more pungently than you could straight-faced. This approach we'll term the "court jester" strategy. You'll recall that kings of yore often hired a clown to tell them truths that might cost a more earnest courtier his head. Since kings in those days did not have Gallup polls, they had to seek truth somewhere. Within limits, court jesters could tell bitter facts in a way to save the royal countenance. ("You are well beloved of your people, sire. That screaming mob outside merely wishes to congratulate you on your imaginative increase in taxes.")

Each of us must use his or her own brand of humor, and then only as much as we feel is suitable. Contriving to inject a pointless joke into an otherwise coherent discourse sounds disjointed and hokey. If you don't instinctively sense humor in a situation, leave it alone.

But consider this. One of the safest and funniest ways to lighten a ponderous speech is the Woody Allen formula. Of an almost ritual simplicity, this consists of a jarring juxtaposition of lofty-familiar, noble-crass, or abstract-concrete. Example: "I'm not sure I believe in an afterlife, but just to make sure, I always carry a change of underwear."

We are not trying here to change you into a stand-up comedian. But if you wish to acquire smoothness and polish in your efforts to explain extraordinary problems to "ordinary" people, some form of wit is almost a necessity. While respecting your subject and your own temperament, stay alert to such opportunities. Humor can help you cast light on obscure or tedious points as no other technique can. At least as important, they can make you an engaging and sympathetic teacher.

All this must be combined with panache and that devilishly difficult-to-cultivate commodity, really convincing false modesty. Authority with simplicity, learning lightly worn—these are your desiderata. Or as we say in the trade, those are the jokes, folks.

Really, I don't mean to take all the fun out of being funny. If humor becomes a duty it is no longer much of a giggle. Just don't forget that showing the wacky, ironic, or anomalous side of things can often situate serious events more poignantly, and thereby heighten the whole impact of your message.

There are, obviously, cases where any kind of humor would shock or offend. It would be hard to see many light refractions in a discourse on leukemia or kidnapping— unless, of course, as a victim yourself, you sought gallows humor. However, if you can, in good taste and with point, inject an illuminating note of wit, do so. The ancient Romans advised, *Castigat ridendo mores* (Improve society —or chastise custom—through laughter). Shakespeare, in Henry IV, would tell of bloody murder, then slot in Falstaff getting bombed and bombastic at a Cheapside pub. As a "serious" humorist, you are in good company.

7. Exploit Slips, Blanks, and Malapropisms

I'm not perfect. Chances are you are only close to it. If Homer can nod, so can we, and we must neither freeze nor fall apart just because we occasionally put our foot in our mouth.

Homer is not the only one among the great to take a public pratfall. Remember Jimmy Carter invoking Hubert

Humphrey as "Hubert Horatio Hornblower"? (Now that *was* Freudian.) Or the 1954 introduction of France's foreign minister, Georges Bidault, as "that fine little French tiger, Georges Bidet"?

Closer to the homespun, there was the *lèse-majesté* faux pas in 1981 of a British businessman congratulating Prince Charles at a banquet on his betrothal to "Lady Jane." He meant Lady Diana. Lady Jane was an old, and tactfully extinct, flame.[1]

Others who are high, if not mighty, have been known to blow their lines. A classic occurred on an Air Canada flight in the early 1970s when an English-speaking pilot, proud but a little nervous at trotting out his newly learned French, warned English-speaking passengers to fasten their seat belts because he was expecting a bit of turbulence ahead. In French he sizzled the intercom with "Mesdames et messieurs, please fasten your seat belts, we are going to have a little masturbation up here."

The story goes on to claim that the same pilot invited French-speaking passengers confronted with a dropping oxygen mask to "pull on the condom." I suspect that at that point the story was sliding into apocrypha. At any rate, at least if you speak French, getting there with Air Canada seems to be half the fun.

Back to work. Boo-boos, to use the technical term, come in all shapes and sizes. I will note only three of the most common ones, to illustrate the wisdom of handling them all with a natural directness.

1. "Oops! How's That Again?" Essay by Roger Rosenblatt, *Time* magazine, March 30, 1981, pp. 75–76.

A significant slip in facts or figures which you instantly recognize, or even remember later in the speech, should be set right. If you told your audience only a minor blooper such as "Our hospital admitted about eight hundred patients a day," whereas the real figure is nine hundred, I would say leave it alone—especially since it's generally less serious to underestimate figures supporting your point than to overstate them. If, on the other hand, you say the name of the hospital chief is Dr. Kildare instead of the proper one, Florence Nightingale, you really must correct yourself.

It's not only that those who know you goofed will appreciate your accuracy. Those who did not spot your mistake will respect your courage in admitting you are fallible. With both knowledgeable and less-knowledgeable people, you gain credibility.

This, you may say, is only common sense. Of course it is. But you would be surprised at how many people are, or have been, afraid of fixing a blooper made in public. As a follower of the Rasputin theory of morality (you must sin first in order to understand and forgive sin), I plead guilty to chickening out occasionally on self-correction, simply because I feared looking silly. Of course, I only did that before writing this book. Having just reread this paragraph, I know I'll never sin again.

Another, sometimes embarrassing problem is malapropisms—the ludicrous misuse of a word ("abnegation" for "abdication"). This can often melt into a Spoonerism ("beery wenches" instead of "weary benches") and, in turn, into a Freudian slip ("My mom pops pills" instead of "My mom gave Pop pills").

The way out of such scrapes, if indeed you realize your mistake with or without help from the audience's guffaws, is quickly to flash through your mind for an apt witticism, preferably one that turns the spotlight off you onto someone or something else likely to amuse your listeners.

Once, for example, I was reminding an audience in Quebec of Canadian Prime Minister Pierre Trudeau's reference to United States–Canada relations as being roughly those you would expect between an elephant and a mouse. Then, still fixated with this image, I went on in the next breath to call Trudeau "Mr. Mouse." The audience exploded, I blushed, for I had obviously stumbled into what they could take as either a sarcasm or a Freudian trap.

Seeing I could not win either way, I apologized for the mixup. Then I added that I must have been thinking of the white mice of a certain rather stiff and doctrinaire Quebec cabinet minister who happened to be a shrink.

It worked. They laughed and forgave.

Another time such evasive tactics only propelled me from the frying pan into the fire. I was trying, as a young prof, to explain to first-year political science students the principle of cabinet solidarity in parliamentary government. Taking the case of a well-known Ottawa defense minister who was disgraced for having allegedly dallied with a blonde who later appeared to have interesting East German antecedents, I innocently explained: "He laid himself open to . . ." (giggles). Then I tried "He violated the principle . . ." (escalating laughter). Finally, frantic for an innuendo-free term to get me off the hook, I stumbled to my instant horror on "He exposed himself . . ." The amphitheater exploded. I turned crimson and incoherent. The kids never did learn about cabinet solidarity. I just could not find words to describe it.

A final and, for readers of this book, horrifying mishap is the memory blank. What on earth can you do if, in spite of Descartes, mental teleprompter and all, you just get lost?

First, you should spin out the point you are making a little longer and hope the lights will go on again in your head. If you drag out your point, some people may think you momentarily a bit dry or windy; but once you find your way, you can always recoup in a brilliant follow-up. If, however, you cannot find your place in that invisible three- or four-part script in your head, do not ramble on for long. Do one of two things.

If the group you are speaking to is small, and you have established a fair amount of intimacy and empathy between you and them, don't hesitate to ask your listeners, quite ingenuously, "Now I got so carried away with that point that I forgot what I promised to tell you next. What was it now?"

Somebody will always speak up to remind you of the next point in the outline you announced so carefully at the outset. You then thank them, pick up your theme with smiling, unblushing aplomb, and press on to impress the audience with your lack of pretension.

You will even feel strangely reassured about your plan. Some people in your audience actually took the trouble to remember it. Now you feel the extra security of knowing they will gladly act as your prompters if you blank out again. For this reason, you won't.

If the audience is larger, though, say over a hundred, you should make a snap decision on whether to go the "Where was I now?" route or whether to resort to your ultimate fail-safe device—that envelope or sheet of paper in your pocket, which carries the skeleton outline of your speech, now your real-life, standby teleprompter.

As it gradually dawns on you that you are indeed lost, and as the cold fear of disgrace begins to creep into your veins, ever so casually slip a couple of fingers into your pocket to fish out your life jacket. Unfold it slowly as you continue to embroider on your last point, slide it up toward your eyes—then, in a quite shameless diversionary move, start a minor coughing spell to sneak a look at it.

I don't mean the coughing fit literally. I do mean that you should resourcefully reach for paper salvation when all else fails. It's not a triumph, of course. But since you never announced from the beginning that you were going to speak entirely without notes, your audience will still find your memory skills extraordinary. They will still find you clever and disciplined, but now a little more vulnerable and human. That won't hurt at all.

What will hurt is a prolonged bluff. If you try for more than a few sentences to meander your way through to your elusive plan, you will start a slow slide into a swamp. You will waffle, worry, and wander until you are spouting words that mean nothing, with a logic only Houdini could unravel. You will suffer, sweat—and sink.

The one and only time I was vain enough and crazy enough to try to swim out of a memory-blank swamp, I became so muddled and unfocused that some listeners thought I had suffered a stroke. I had. A stroke of madness which I now consider a stroke of luck. For like a scalded cat, I'm cured forever of self-indulgent showing off. Except when I'm skiing—and even then I use poles.

8. Foresee and Finesse Hecklers

One of the most enjoyable opportunities of public speaking is heckling: the chance that somebody may think you are speaking nonsense, and say so aloud while you are performing. It's an opportunity because it gives you a new occasion to discover the richness of your mind, your Gibraltar-steady nerves, and your gift for suave, or at least apt, repartee.

Well, that's the optimistic view. Hecklers, if smarter or luckier than you, can also unhinge you and reduce you to tongue-tied ridicule.

We have ways, however, of making you talk—and helping you to think quickly before you talk. The ways are psychological training, and prepared solutions to foreseeable traps. Your psychological prepping comes from reminding yourself, before the speech, of three trump cards every speaker holds.

First, you are the one the audience came to hear. Any intruders, especially rude or heavy-footed ones, will earn the interloper hostility and you sympathy. Second, you know your subject probably better than any or most of the people in the room—and almost certainly better than any heckler. If he were so smart, you can tell yourself, why didn't your hosts invite him instead of you? If indeed your hosts invited both of you and the guy is butting in out of turn, the audience will think he is a boor. All you have to do in that case is smile long-sufferingly and wash him down the drain with some perfidious words such as "I'm sure we are all eager to hear your views, my friend. If you would just not mind letting me finish my time, you can seal my doom at your leisure." Or something to that effect.

A third reason you should feel serene about interruptions is a practical one. You control the microphone. This automatically allows you to outshout the buttinskies, without even appearing to shout. Even if there is no mike, you still hold the floor—as often as not a raised one, from which you can glower, lift blasé eyebrows, or if necessary spit down on your tormentor.

All of this, you'll agree, is immensely reassuring. Whenever you tremble before a speech at the prospect of hecklers, recite these built-in advantages to yourself, and you will simmer down. No, you will feel positively masterful. You will gnash your teeth in expectation.

What about prepared solutions? Good repartee, like awesome improvisation, rests on painstaking homework. Ninety percent of all quotable repartee seems to have been premeditated. It's not a matter of lightning-like genius, it's a question of repertoire.

Distressing news? Only if you truly believed that every one of Winston Churchill's or Adlai Stevenson's anthology-bound quips leaped to their lips in the heat of the fray. Many of these masters' *bons mots* did, of course. I like to think that when Churchill heard in the Commons that the Greek Prime Minister was called Plasteras, his muttered "I trust he does not have feet of clay as well" was a genuine flash of, er, astuteness.

However, Churchill, like Stevenson and any truly candid public speaker, avowed that he collected retorts for years, then waited for a chance to slip each one into whatever serviceable slot the fates brought him. History does not tell exactly how far Richard Sheridan, the eighteenth-century British playwright-parliamentarian, went in saving up stinging putdowns, but it's hard to believe he did not whip off the following all-time winner on the spur of the moment. When an adversary in the House hissed that Sheridan was such a rogue that he would die either on the gallows or of some foul disease, Sheridan shot back, "That will depend entirely, Mr. Speaker, on whether I embrace the honorable member's principles or his mistress."[2]

A similarly cutting retort from ancient times came from the great Cicero, a speaker so renowned for his rapier tongue that Caesar himself collected his witticisms. When the snobbish aristocrat Q. Metellus Nepos tried to put Cicero down by sneering "Who was your father?" Cicero singed him with the scorcher: "I can scarcely ask you the same question, since your mother has made it rather difficult to answer."[3] Any guy with a name like Q. Metellus Nepos deserved something like that, wouldn't you say?

Another in Sheridan's and Cicero's class was nineteenth-century Conservative statesman Benjamin Disraeli, who alternated as British Prime Minister with his Liberal arch-rival William Gladstone. The pinched and prissy

2. Sheridan's barb, like many *répliques,* was good enough to be claimed by several plausible wits—among them John Wilkes, the Earl of Sandwich, and Benjamin Franklin.

3. *Cicero: Selected Political Speeches,* cited in Introduction by translator Michael Grant, Penguin Classics, London, 1969, p. 14.

Gladstone interrupted Disraeli to claim he was talking so loosely about "disaster" and "catastrophe" that he was stripping the words of all meaning. Disraeli riposted "Of course I know how these words differ in meaning. If my honorable friend (Gladstone) were to fall into the Thames, one could speak of a 'disaster.' But were someone to pull him out, one would have to term it a 'catastrophe.'"

That's the big leagues of vituperation. Not many of us have opportunities—or enemies—worthy of such class, but we can, in our small worlds, draw spirit and imagination from the great masters' examples. We can, as most of them have done, make a habit of writing out three or four juicy repartees which obviously sensitive passages of our talk might call forth. Then, if we are challenged at these points, we can start, at least, with a fall-back answer.

If the heckler points his or her sally to a tack which you can exploit with a more telling rejoinder, by all means zap the rascal with your fresher inspiration. However, just having in your quiver a few comments which might fit a controversial point, or even a person or type of person you expect trouble from, can give you peace of mind—indeed, a more inventive mind.

List your adversaries, and list their strongest points. Imagine a few devastating formulas. Learn them. Then use them if and when needed. Most of the time, your tormentors will try to embarrass you with superficial courtesy as they mock or query your contradictions or misinformation. For these polite intruders, your best defense is to listen carefully and sympathetically (even if you are boiling inside, you should smile as though intrigued by the remote possibility the chap might have a point worth interrupting the speech your audience came to hear). Then, as you listen, try to sense your questioner's Achilles heel (a wrong fact, an imprudent judgment, a contradiction of his own, or one with his allies). Once you know what he wants, give him only what you want. This might be a polite correction, a quip that turns the tables on him, or even a humorous or instructive, very brief, fable.

Whichever technique you use for the ostensibly respectful questioner, bite back quickly, but with rarely more than gentle irony. Answer in kind, but with a little more courtesy than your questioner. If you come off sounding ruder than your questioner—beware of heavy sarcasm—you will seem clumsy and frightened. Even if you are right on the facts, you may lose the contest for your listeners' sympathy.

The way to keep an audience on your side, obviously, is *never* to lose your self-control. If you are dealing with a really raucous and offensive heckler, this still allows you to get tougher without losing dignity or audience. In fact, if you can promptly and authoritatively put some lout in his place, they'll love you for it. He bleats from the back of the hall some inelegance about barnyard excrement? Cut him down with "Now, sir, that you've told us the name of your organization, we'll put you on our mailing list."

Mocking, but harmless to your reputation as a class act. Weave your own witticisms for the kinds of situations and people you deal with. Build up a lifetime repertoire of quips for recurring opportunities, and add to these a few tailor-made ones for the predictable needs of each talk. Then have fun.

A last consoling quote to boost your stage ego before

the huddled masses below. Think of potential hecklers in the way that, William Hazlitt reported, Daniel Defoe thought of some of his contemporaries: "He says there were a hundred thousand stout country-fellows in his time ready to fight to the death against Popery, without knowing whether Popery was a man or a horse."

Hecklers are like mobs. Let them know that if they attack you, the horse's mouth, they will end up as the other end of the horse.

9. Appeal to Higher Instincts

Let's leave the barnyard for the ethereal realms of the spirit. Much of our quackery above reduces eloquence to its mere technical level—to the low, if necessary, apprenticeship of craft. But as cabinetmaking is more than sawing and hammering, so fine rhetoric must rise above breathing, joking, and retorts. To dig deep in the rich ore of oratory, to "master the English language," as did Churchill, "and send it into battle," you must link your prose about practicalities to the finest values you can discern in your audience.

This strategy of tying the prosaic to the poetic, the concrete to the abstract, the low to the lofty, is the reverse of the Woody Allen high-low technique of humor we discussed earlier in this chapter. Its impact on your audience is not exactly the opposite of humorous, but it is sobering and galvanizing. Humor relaxes and creates perspectives; it probes the wisdoms of incongruity. Dancing between the humble-tangible and the noble-spiritual tends

to seize your listeners' hearts. It incites them to a deeper
meditation, then to consequent action.

We are talking here about courage, kindness, generosity, love, sharing, sacrifice, honesty—the fundamental
fibers of a decent society. What we are seeking now, as we
ponder the mood in which we want to leave our audience,
is how to illuminate such virtues. Your audience at least la-
tently displays such virtues, and you, the speaker, would
like to bring them out.

For example? You are a bookseller telling high-school
kids what good books can offer them. First you touch on
the obvious benefit of learning that you know they can relate
to: the dreadful, materialist, career-oriented motivation—
reading books gets you jobs. Distasteful as you may find
such a pitch, we all know that's about what you need first
in this ad-crazy civilization to get many students' attention.
Having engaged the kids on the job front, you then ease
them into broader and higher considerations: the enrich-
ment of their spirit, their ability to live and taste a good
life. You lead them to Tolstoy's reflection on "How much
land does a man need?" You tell them quietly that jobs are
fine and necessary to put bread on the table. But what
about a jug of wine? By wine you mean your mind's and
heart's skill in savoring the texture of human relationships,
of weighing the warmths and wiles of your fellows. You
sum up by saying that a book-stretched mind can lead to
an examined life—the only kind worth living.

The students, who started out with you on a money-
grubbing itinerary, find at the end that you have led them
tenderly into a voyage about their indivisible happiness.
You have reminded them delicately, through concrete ex-

ample, of how wisdom brings us closer into harmony with our world and its essential ingredient, other human beings.

You could do the same in a less contrived way if your audience were Sunday sailors you were talking to about navigation. Naturally, you, the Ancient Mariner, would teach them how a beam reach would tack you better through a certain tide than a close haul. But if you are the kind of seafarer who glimpses beyond tillers and trade winds to the lonely grandeurs of man against the sea—the spiritual dimension of sailing—you would find a way of linking your lessons to the meaning of going down to the sea in ships.

I'm not pleading that every one of your speeches should end in a mawkish harangue or a sermon. I'm merely saying that what lifts an ordinary spiel to the plateau of eloquence is your ability to use any theme to bring your audience, and yourself, into closer communion with your topic's underlying meanings.

If you can see such an opening, and use it to articulate the ideals that unite you, your listeners, and your subject in a universe of admirable values, you will have scaled the heights.

If mountain-climbing scares you, however, or merely tires you, or if you see no particular mountain to climb, read on. We'll end our in-flight service with three very down-to-earth hints.

10. Play the Applause

What is this manipulative horror? Play the applause? Trifle with people's emotions, treat them as automatons

from whom you can elicit Pavlovian slobberings? Not quite
—but a skilled speaker can draw and control applause to
an almost uncanny degree. It's genteelly called "milking"
the audience. Max Atkinson of Oxford University has
made a brilliant study of applause techniques of well-
known British and U.S. politicians. He catalogues tricks
that can transform an average speaker into a crowd-stirring
star.[4]

Atkinson believes that people rarely clap for a politician spontaneously. Politicians excite nearly all their audience reactions by fishing for applause through specific rhetorical devices. These, in a kind of ritual code, set up
vibrations (think of one tuning fork making another re-
sound) which almost irresistibly move listeners to crack
the tension with applause.

You will recognize some of these ploys as we describe
them. You will remember times when a speaker set up a
rhythm, lifted you to a pitch, or built a contradiction,
which cried out for you to break it by making a bloody
fool of yourself.

Read on, and forgive yourself for being such a dupe.
Besides, your jerking knees may only have indicated that
you are musical.

The first four of the following devices are Atkinson's;
I've tacked on a few more that sometimes work:

a) *Repetition and Sign-off:* a series of sentences similar in style. These I think of as an escalating cadence, a

4. Robert Eagle, "Why Are Politicians So Charismatic . . ."
New Scientist, October 2, 1980, pp. 33–35.

hammer-blow effect which nails home a point, as we discussed earlier. I regret to tell you that our old friend the hypnotic trilogy seems to wreak its black magic here as well. You can pull off four, even five, even six, hammer-blow sentences without losing your headlong music. But three, as in most things mystical and artistic, seem to carry a special, compelling force.

If you are doing this in the middle of a speech, it's best to start with a high intonation, then drift slightly downward as you reach your punch line. Remember Ronald Reagan during the 1980 presidential campaign: "I don't want Jimmy Carter's job. . . . That's not what I want (pause, the dropped voice) . . . I want to be President of the United States." Reagan used a variation on this device when he was trying to climb his way out of his alleged inability to tell a recession from a depression: "Recession is when your neighbor loses his job . . . depression is when you lose your job . . . and recovery is when Jimmy Carter loses his job."

The late John Diefenbaker, Canada's Prime Minister from 1957 to 1963, was a gleeful conductor of a crowd's emotions. Like Reagan, he loved to stick a stiletto in his victims: "The Liberal government has declared a war on poverty. It's put Tom Kent in charge. Well, at $25,000 a year [this was a long time back] he's won *his* war on poverty."

If you are pulling this trick near the final crescendo of your speech, you can raise or lower your voice's pitch to fit the mood you wish to end with: a higher pitch for the upbeat, a lower one for the solemn.

A variant on multi-sentence repetition is alliteration.

Used sparingly and with discernment, it can reinforce a point, heighten attention, and spark laughter and/or applause. Denouncing John Foster Dulles's foreign policy, Tennessee Governor Frank Clement, a master of Ciceronian style, teased: "Foster fiddles, frets, fritters and flits." That worked because it was apt, funny, and one of only a few alliterations in that 1956 speech. Vice-president Spiro Agnew gave alliteration a bad name for a long time by using it too often and with stretched meanings: his tormentors in the eastern media came off as "the nattering nabobs of negativism." (What he meant, obviously, was "simpering satraps of cynicism.")[5]

b) *Contrast:* This technique, found Atkinson, is the most common one for triggering applause in the middle of a speech. Here you set up not a rising tension, but a Ping-Pong tension. To make sure your audience feels like breaking the tension, you must make your contrast black and white. If you are too subtle, they may miss your point and leave you hanging.

Examples? Here's a good clear contrast, which got British left-wing parliamentary master Anthony Benn three bursts in under two minutes: "We shall find two or three million demoralized, long-term unemployed who have to be put back to work in factories *not that Hitler* has bombed *but that* [Prime Minister Margaret] *Thatcher* and [Secretary of State for Industry Sir Keith] *Joseph* have

5. I am indebted to Frank Morrow's splendid essay, "The Decline and Fall of Eloquence" for several examples here. See *Time* magazine, August 18, 1980, pp. 55–56.

closed" (applause, heightened by the charming insinuation that Thatcher and Joseph were somehow more cruel than Hitler).

Benn went on: "I am waiting for us to say more often that some things are *right* . . . and some things are *wrong* (applause) . . . that it is wrong to cut down on money for *kidney machines* and spend five billion on a new *Polaris submarine* (applause) . . ."

c) *Talking During Applause:* a common stunt for egomaniacs trafficking in false modesty. Affecting to be unaware of the thunderous approval crashing down around them, some speakers just press on . . . or appear to. "You can say almost anything you want," advises Atkinson, "repeat yourself, or just waffle. But if you keep talking you give the impression that you were not really fishing for applause in the first place and that you are so popular that you are being drowned by your audience's enthusiasm."

Dastardly. But even lovable Johnny Carson resorts to this, his "premature" attempts to break through applause shattering his words into an aw-shucks stutter of becoming naturalness. In Hollywood and Vegas, they all do it. The greater your known ego, the more they'll lap it up. People love to see a flash of naïveté in the great. It's toga-touching again.

d) *Offbeat Breathing:* Inflicting on us something like the dubious joys of *coitus interruptus,* some speakers inject pauses in the damnedest places to heighten anticipation and attentiveness. Personally, I find this pompous, but Jimmy Carter did not, and he used it to good effect: "In recent years (pause) expanding (pause) Soviet power (pause) has increasingly (pause) penetrated (pause) beyond (pause) the North Atlantic area."

TV editors have noted that Carter's mid-sentence pauses, plus his racing past the end of one sentence into the next one, forced networks to give him more airtime. They could not logically cut him in mid-sentence; and between sentences he left them no time.

If you see a written text for a fairly good political orator (they can only be *fairly* good if they rely on a text . . .) you will note how telegraphic their phrases become when they want to do a little milking. According to Democratic Party experts whom Atkinson consulted, bursts of seven to nine words are ideal to sustain tension. They also offer more occasions to break it with applause when it becomes intolerable.

Next time you hear a politician start the old staccato ploy, plug your ears. He is getting ready to recruit you as an extra for his next noisy mob-scene.

In addition to Atkinson's fundamentals, you will recognize these old standbys for giving your listeners itchy palms:

- *Rhetorical Questions:* Was it really necessary to mention these?
- *Supplied-Answer Questions:* Do you want to learn all about these? Of course you do. And now you have.
- *Irony:* In these last three subsections, you are being run through a standard end-of-speech acceleration. Now you are all ready for our little

wrap-up on wrap-ups, otherwise known as perorations.

11. End on a Peak

"Leave 'em laughin'," went the old show-biz saw. Not
every speech is funny, but the idea of leaving your listeners
in a mood of excitement, mobilization, or just thought-
fulness is not a bad one for any talk you give.

How do you achieve this? How can you lift your audience to a summit of interest and involvement as you finish?

Many of the technical tricks we have already looked
at in this chapter may fit the bill. The just-discussed mechanics of milking applause can help especially. For an
upbeat, or just uplifting, ending, the crescendo or decre-
scendo of hammer-blow final phrases can win you a cheap
triumph anytime. It is important to remember, though, that
these are merely the devices of a certain polish, or professional smoothness. They can easily degenerate into charlatanism. Using the tricks without common sense, generosity,
and a real care for your topic may leave you with a clever
little essay in demagogy. What we are after here is eloquence.

Eloquence begins in the heart: it is concern for your
cause or issue. Then it must filter through a disciplined
mind, following a method which marshals ideas convincingly. Finally, as your mastery of method frees your
thoughts and leads your mind to improvise, you should return to the heart. You should end by caring a great deal
about your subject and your listeners.

As you reach toward the last five or even ten percent of your speech, you should open your heart to your audience. During the analytical part of your talk, you have had to concentrate on giving with your mind—dredging up ideas, refining them, formulating them. Now, your case made, you should try to channel your listeners' emotions toward accepting with their hearts what you hope they have agreed to in their minds.

This all sounds preachy and flimsy. But becoming a technician of rhetoric is not the same as being an orator. If you do not radiate truth, sanity, even a lucid idealism, people may be dazzled but they won't follow you.

However humble your theme—unless you are called on only to recite raw data—think of your goal as sending your audience out to right some wrong, to build a better world. That world may be higher-quality automobile parts (that's how the Japanese do it), more loving care for the aged, the eyesight problems of coyotes, or the various configurations of Hollywood casting couches. Whatever the topic, give a damn and show it. Then your audience will.

Do we need another book on the fine art of faking sincerity? Perhaps. But that's not what we have in mind here.

12. Land on Time

Our friends the pilots, when they are not announcing turbulence or other amusements, often speak of ETA. That's Estimated Time of Arrival.

Punctuality is not just the courtesy of kings. Ending on time is your last chance to tell your listeners that you respect them. If you are given forty-five minutes, take forty-five, not fifty or sixty minutes. If you have five, take five.

Since by now you are winging your way as cockily as an inebriated eagle, you need not fear an occasional glance at your watch. Indeed, when you look at your watch *only,* you craftily remind your audience that, my God, you are up there all alone, naked except for your little quartz Seiko.

Use it. Begin your landing approach in good time to meet the coffee or cocktail hour that everyone is lusting for. Then touch down in a gorgeous pinpoint landing just when you said you would.

I'm only repeating what Miss Grumpypuss told you about the three rules of public speaking when you were in high school:

> Stand up.
> Speak up.
> Shut up.

Welcome back to earth. You've won your wings.

Eloquence is thought on fire.

—WILLIAM JENNINGS BRYAN

PART THREE

DIGESTING WHEN AND WHY: THE AERODYNAMICS OF ELOQUENCE

Choice words and measured phrase, above the reach
Of ordinary men; a stately speech;
Such as grave livers do in Scotland use.

—WILLIAM WORDSWORTH, *Resolution and Independence*

CHAPTER TEN

When Not To Wing It

Up to now, we've packed your brain with new tricks, new drills, perhaps even a few new insights, for flying solo onstage. In Part One you learned a method for noteless public speaking; in Part Two you soaked up exercises and advice on how to get winging it into your blood.

This Part Three aims to help you rise above the skills of a mere technician of oratory. It is designed to anchor your new understanding and mastery in a deeper outlook on public speaking. It seeks not to train you more, but to make you assess the place of eloquence in your life and society.

Do you really need this entrenching philosophy? Must you go beyond "plumbing" to "poetry"? Frankly, you can survive very well without it. But like France's great philos-

opher-aviator, Antoine de Saint-Exupéry, you can have a
lot more fun flying noteless if you start the habit of *thinking* what you're doing as well as *doing* it.

Besides, as an *aficionado* of three-part Cartesian teleprompter plans, can you possibly pass up seeing how we
round off this do-it-yourself handbook? Now that you mention it, I'd say we have run through a plan of chronological
utilitarianism: telling you first the basic technique you
needed to know, then moving on to tutor you in the system's
refinements. Finally, in this third, driving-it-home section,
we want to send you off reflecting on what you've picked
up. We want to help you *enjoy* how winging it can make
you fly high in the world of deadly, stilted, written-and-
read tedium that passes almost everywhere for speech-
ifying.

In this section, we start in Chapter Ten by putting
winging it in context: listing occasions (there are some)
when you need not, or ought not, wing it. Chapter Eleven
puts you back on track with a recap of why and when you
should get on with winging it. Finally, as we float you
quickly to book's end, Chapter Twelve hints of hope that
winging it, and its clever disciples such as you, can get the
English-speaking world airborne again (if ever it was).

An immodest pretension? Don't be so shy. After reading all this, you should believe the sky's the limit. On then,
first with our suitably short chapter on times you need not
wing it.

This book has dealt with shyness, and with a specific
technique for overcoming it by talking noteless in public.

Speaking without paper, like marrying without a license, suggests something bold as well as practical. It even offers a similar, faintly sinful, thrill. People in North America long ago lost the skill of casual eloquence, and when somebody like you helps bring it back while other speakers plod on riveted to the written word, you feel smarter than they. Even a little smug.

Let's admit it cheerfully: we all enjoy nurturing a mild superiority complex. If you don't take yourself too seriously, such an attitude can be classed as healthy. Call it confidence.

Speakers of every kind need plenty of that. Whether as a "speaker" you address twenty million people on TV, two thousand in a convention hall, or two in an office bull-session, you want to feel in control. First, you need to be in control of yourself. Then you have a chance at being in control of your audience—even if that means your listeners end up only respecting you and your ideas, not buying your viewpoint.

To put this book's confidence-building advice in context, let's admit that the system it outlines has limits. Knowing that, you, the user, can target its use to purposes it really works well for. Winging it, we've seen, can hearten you to breathe authority and spontaneity into nearly all of your public speaking. Yet there are some times when you ought to keep a grip on yourself, and your subject, by sticking to a text. Our examples run from lofty to lowly— not always for you to identify with literally, but perhaps, in similarly untragic vein, to help you draw your own common-sense parallels:

1. When Speaking for Posterity

Are you the President of the United States? I don't advise you to wing your State-of-the-Union Address. Are you merely the Vice-president of the United States, bored with the "warm pitcher of spit" that is your job and plotting an ego-rewarding replay of the Gettysburg Address? Plan your place in history, assure your fame in the anthologies, by drafting a short, heart-lifting speech that kiddies from now to eternity can cite as spit with polish.

Are you (perhaps it's time to broaden this book's market a little) only the winner of this year's Nobel Prize for Literature? Do as Alexander Solzhenitsyn did: undam a shimmering, silver river of prose that can be bound in vellum and handed as a graduation present to English majors.

The same stay-with-your-typewriter approach is the right on for symposia, colloquia, and other orgies of academic incest. Here you're expected to speak for "publication" in obscure journals—failing which you "perish" as a prof. Likewise—if you live neither in White House nor ivory tower—might you consider drafting a formal testimonial. When Joe the Janitor retires after fifty years or Brainy Brenda wins her school's top prize, his or her moment of honor can glow for years in a rereadable tribute or traditional scroll. Farewells and triumphs deserve gracious improvisations; but that's no reason to deny the day's hero the more lasting narcissism of a souvenir he can frame.

2. When It's a Life-or-Death Issue

Egypt and Israel, like the United States and the Soviet Union, link their capital cities with a twenty-four-hour-a-day Telex hotline. When General Motors and the United Auto Workers try to avoid a strike, they exchange position papers, detailing maximum and minimum terms. When the Pope lays down his views on abortion or mercy killing, he publishes an encyclical.

Why? Why don't presidents and popes wing it by phone, radio, or TV? Because, obviously, lives are at stake. Lives, jobs, power bases, vital interests, moral and political authority.

An example a little closer to home? The PR statement by a company just caught watering its beer or leaking nuclear radiation. If your firm or group finds itself pants-down, the surest way to cover its assurances may be a cunningly crafted written statement.

You seek peace with the press? Hacks vobiscum, pax vobiscum. Write something—c-a-r-e-f-u-l-l-y—get it out, then get out of the way while the press gives you whatever you deserve. If you really must stonewall, use wallpaper you might enjoy in your jail cell.

Whatever your line of work—teaching, sales, law, politics, management, or frog-jumping championships—once in a while you face a crisis when you don't want to risk your career or your family's happiness on a miscue. If you tremble at the make-or-break stakes, and believe you must take a distilled, subtly shaded position, don't wing it. Write it.

Should you have a photographic memory, you can still make a splash with your audience by learning your speech by heart. More likely, like most of us, you have a sieve in your head instead of a Hasselblad. If that's the case, forget about vulgar display and read as much life into your do-or-die document as you can.

For the life-or-death stuff we're talking about here, theatrical effect is the least of your problems. Your reason for writing being to ward off disaster, there is no shame in reading a clear, sober text—which, we take for granted, will also be unflinchingly honest and fair.[1]

3. When Imprecise Language May Cost You Friends or Money

Take your friends first. If they are friends, and not just acquaintances, contacts, or some guys you met in a bar ten minutes ago, they should allow you two or three really worthwhile misunderstandings per year. But once in a while, if you are an officeholder in your country, city, or organization, you will offend some sector of your constituency. You may just have wanted to stir things up. If you

1. Apart from stage actors, the only orator of modern times known to memorize entire speeches was Charles de Gaulle. Before he died from an overdose of chocolate éclairs, he used to dazzle TV and platform audiences by delivering twenty minutes of polished prose without a note in sight. Since he refused to wear glasses in public, a real teleprompter was impractical—and, as a burden while walking on water, no doubt hazardous.

mainly managed to wound old allies, though, you may be wise to apologize and/or set the record straight in the media with a fairly formal "clarification." Again, ideally, you should not read such a text. It should be short enough to memorize, and if that is very short, so much the better.

If you want to swim out of hot water with class, you should glide as far as you can freestyle, without paper-shuffling to betray insincerity or lingering guilt. By drowning your formal, memorized segments in a more spontaneous beginning and ending, you can pull off your *mea culpa* both safely and convincingly.

The same goes for lovers' spats, of which I trust you still enjoy a few. Romeo and Cyrano were not above using Shakespeare and Rostand as their writers for dicey declarations. You may, without disgrace, decide to do the same—preferably plagiarizing yourself. If you do, of course, you will violate the prudent rake's advice for avoiding trouble with mistresses—"do right and do not write"—but you may shape a sounder reconciliation, or a smoother escape.

One occasion of the heart where a script seems smarter and smarter is the marriage or live-together contract. With palimony blocking every decent rogue's exit from alimony, you may forget whispering flowery ambiguities to your beloved. If you really want to share bed and breakfast with her or him, split the loot on paper first, and avoid fighting over the Tony Bennett records later.

Even if only money, not friendship, is at stake, you must often use pen and paper. Whether buying a car, a house, or an unpretentious little yacht, you ought to get the bargain in writing.

Caveat emptor—let the buyer beware—is the oldest and best economic advice in the world. If you are making a pitch to buy or sell anything pricier than a paper clip, reassure all concerned by putting the deal on paper. You can always back up your arguments in an improvised commentary on point-form notes, but your text will make the deal look—and be—better-prepared than strictly oral appeals. These usually smack of being off-the-cuff, and often lead to being foot-in-mouth.

4. When You Want the Press To Quote You Accurately

"Don't get it right, get it written," goes an old saying nastily ascribed to journalistic cynics. Do not believe the worst of your fallible friends in the media. Not all of them thirst to destroy reputations by twisting or inventing quotes. As Goethe (or conceivably Lou Grant) said: "Don't leap to see conspiracy at every turn; you must never underestimate the likelihood of stupidity."

Despite their victims' calumnies, most journalists—like most dentists or carpenters—are neither sadists nor imbeciles. They *try* to do a competent, conscientious job. But if accurate quotes of your speech matter a lot, give the reporters and yourself a break by handing them a résumé of your main passages.

If you need to help newsmen catch a deadline, give them this text in advance. Be open, as well as flexible: entitle it "notes for a speech" to leave yourself room for asides, updates, examples, reasonable variations, and deathbed repentances. But remember, if your words land you in hot water, your text may prove either life jacket or straitjacket. Weasely protests of "misquotes" never endear. Denying your own written words risks tagging you as a liar or a clown.

Never, never hand out a full text unless, in all modesty, you believe the whole thing is worth quoting. Skip the ritual intro ("how pleased I am to be here among my fellow chicken-sexers"), which you should be bright enough, and courteous enough, to improvise to fit your listeners' mood. Stick to your core arguments, preferably listing them in point form—but use full, flowing, quotable sentences.

Do you want the TV and radio people to cover you live, instead of interviewing you before or after your talk? You can help them out (and sometimes ever so tactfully target their coverage) by pointing out to them ahead of time three or four points you think might get you—and them—on the evening news bulletin. If the news people are worth their salt, they will sublimely ignore your advice. But you can try: the TV crew cannot leave on their lights for a forty-minute speech, and your unmeddlesome guidance just might lend a hand.

As we noted earlier, your choice in all these games lies between winning your audience in the hall and snatching at the larger public of newspapers, TV, and radio. Let influence, not ego, decide.

5. When Your Talk Is a Laundry List

Not every speech you give aims to startle the indifferent, shake the skeptical, or sway the unwashed.

Sometimes you just want to pass along facts or figures. For this, the laundry-list oration, you might as well get the stuff right by writing it, then reading it.

A good example might be a school principal introducing thirty different teachers to a parent-teacher meeting, sketching cradle-to-foible biographies for each. Another would be the treasurer of the SPCA rattling off for his directors the numbers of stray ocelots corralled by the dogcatcher last year, then tacking on month-by-month bonuses paid for chewed-up fingers. Whatever your raw material, if it's mainly a recital of details your audience wants, lay it on them off the paper, not off the cuff. Your job hangs on being thorough and reliable? Don't fumble the facts by grandstanding.

Doing such a workmanlike job does not mean you can't punctuate your data with little flashes of wit. If the audience seems to welcome it, and you feel the urge, you can inject grace into the most tedious of texts. You can achieve this by expressiveness, organization, or asides.

Drama critics used to say that Charles Laughton could make a telephone book sing like Shakespeare. You might think more in terms of Woody Allen or Jerry Falwell, but the idea is the same: breathe life into your material by thinking about it and caring about it as you speak. A radio producer once taught me a good trick for making words leap off the page: "Don't *read* me your story; *tell* me about it as you read."

You can also make long recitals less boring by marshaling your facts in appealing order. Group your data in categories which mirror more down-to-earth concerns, hint at a nobler mood, or focus with humor. Say you have to list twenty-five honorary pallbearers at the funeral of your rapacious great-uncle. You could name first those who revered the old devil from afar, then those who worked more closely with him, and finally those intimates about whom you just barely refrain from noting that familiarity bred contempt.

Another list-lightener is the aside. To pace rather than intrude, an aside must match the subject and the way you feel about it. If the occasion is joyful, build on the audience's good humor. If it's tragic, add only dignified grace notes, and sparingly. If the theme and moment are emotionally neutral, follow your instinct about a bit of gentle irony: as a YMCA secretary reporting on flagging numbers of recruits, you might get away with citing a "modest increase, very modest, from two hundred new members to one hundred seventy-five."

These are only embroidery to make your reliance on reading less obvious. The point remains that, unless you can readily memorize large chunks of raw information, you should not try to dazzle your listeners with total recall. If the latter turns out to be less than total, they may not recall you as a speaker.

As you can see, the times you truly need a text are few —the historic, the life-or-death, the cash-or-caring, the newsworthy, the data-drenched. In fact, as you gain practice at winging it, you will be able to handle even many of those "momentous moments" without paper crutches.

Meanwhile, you face countless less alarming chances

to try your wings. Let's review next why and when you should hone your new flying skills. You are now licensed to take off without notes and with fear as your friendly co-pilot. It won't hurt to shove you gently once more into the cockpit.

For it is feeling and force of imagination that makes us eloquent.

—QUINTILIAN

CHAPTER ELEVEN

Why (Again) and When To Fly

Our previous chapter was not meant to wean you back to reading speeches. It aimed only to caution you that, once in a rare while, you can do better with a text. You nearly always should keep a strong bias in favor of winging it. Winging it, in the end, will give you what no amount of reading speeches can offer: an eloquence truly yours, thus credibility, and a lasting cure for shyness.

But in case you need a last spot of spine-stiffening, we'll recap here the reasons why you ought to fly noteless. Then we'll nudge you to pluck up your courage and soon do what birds do, bees do, and even pilots do: practice.

1. Written Speech Makes Rotten Speech

Writing is the natural enemy of speech. Unless you can write dialogue like Neil Simon, learn it like Ingrid

Bergman, and speak it like Richard Burton, a text read verbatim will capture you but lose your audience.

Let's see how and why by looking at the speech itself, the audience, and the speaker.

a) *The Words:* Sir Francis Bacon counseled four centuries ago: "It is generally better to deal by speech than by letter." He also advised: "Reading maketh a full man; conference a ready man; and writing an exact man." If you dare to speak at all in front of others, you must be smart enough to do your homework—to be already the "full man" who has read. As between Bacon's other two options —speaking ("conference") and writing—speaking requires that you choose to be more quick-witted and spontaneous ("ready") than, as a writer, you would be "exact."

Does choosing spontaneity over precision mean you can be sloppy about facts, figures, or wording? Of course not. It simply means that, speaking, you can communicate on more levels than in writing. Writing relies only on words; speaking engages words, but also quality of voice, timing, expression, body language, mood, and presence.

In Chapter Ten, we talked of occasions when precision should outweigh all these factors. If you know your subject and mind, however, you should try most times to use the extra channels of understanding that rhetoric opens. They multiply your chances of making an impact on your audience's intellect and, especially, emotions.

What if you can afford a ghost-writer? Well, if he is John Kennedy's Ted Sorensen or Richard Nixon's William Safire, maybe. And then only if you can pass yourself off as bright enough really to have written the speech yourself—

and can speak it as though such lofty phrases roll off your tongue every time you ask for the French dressing.

There are just two problems with using a speech writer: the speech writer and you. About one ghost in a thousand owns the versatility and ear to build cadences around another person's mouth. It's not just a matter of matching the speaker's brains and culture. It's matching his style, taste, whims, and ego. Even if you, the ghost, think you can fix in formaldehyde your speaker's personality, you run the risk of aping him. In the days when I rented words to various politicians, the guy I caught most faithfully was the one I had the most arguments with about nit-picky phrases and constructions: fidelity became caricature.

The double-jeopardy risk of the ghost is that, if you make your average speaker sound like a genius, the audience may laugh at him; if you copy the clever man to the point of parody, he may get mad at you. In either case, your career will be short.

The other unhappy partner in these two-person speeches is the speaker. As I've hinted, and as you knew very well anyway, about the only people who can read a speech to full effect are trained actors. You may recall old Hollywood hand Ronald Reagan at the July 1980 Republican Convention. In an otherwise dreary roster of speakers, and even with a speech that did not soar off the page, he uplifted or appalled—but gripped. Reagan only did B-movies and kitchen commercials, you say? Do not mock Bonzo and Borax. They claim their place in the destiny of nations.

Even Ted Kennedy, at the Democratic Convention a

few days later, started with two decades on the rostrum. Then he holed up for hours in his hotel to rehearse with a videotape recorder and staff. His read speech was acclaimed as perhaps his best ever—but it was patched together by a stable of the finest scribblers and broken in as an off-Broadway artist would rote-learn a play. You may have this kind of talent; you may have some experience. Chances are you won't often have this kind of time and high-priced coaching.

It's not even enough to be an instinctive actor. You may be superb at improvising theatrics, but you may prove a dud with a text. In this category come to mind such live-wire stump speakers, but boring speech readers, as India's Indira Gandhi, Cuba's Fidel Castro, and Canada's Pierre Trudeau.

There are times, of course, when a politician may wish to be dull. As George Orwell pointed out in his classic essay "Politics and the English Language," obfuscation, evasion, and ambiguity keep as many politicians in power as bayonets or ballot boxes. Most speakers, however, want to be reasonably clear, indeed punchy. For them, rehearsing a written speech out loud is as necessary a discipline as playing scales is for a concert pianist.

The sneaky way out of reading a speech is the good old four- by six-inch flip card. Is this not a reasonable middle course between the sleep-producing reading lesson and the off-the-dock dive without a text? Not really. Again the problem lies with both practice and practitioners.

In themselves, flip cards break the flow of your discourse. You may well move your audience by the smoothly sculpted paragraphs you build on each card, but as soon as you seem to be flying, you must stop again to glance at your idiot cards. Can you guess why people call them idiot cards? You shatter the magic—the illusion that you have mastered your material. You jar your public back to earth by constantly pointing to your crutches. As a reminder that you are perhaps not, after all, divinely inspired, these intrusive little cards are like hiccups in the middle of a sermon.

The problem turns to farce when speakers either mix up their cards in the wrong sequence, drop them on the platform, or shuffle them nervously. Maybe you can palm cards with the out-of-the-cuff adroitness of a Mississippi riverboat gambler. If not, you will distract, not conquer, your listeners. Drop the cards (at home); keep your audience.

b) *The Audience:* Apart from paper-shuffling distractions, audiences face one congenital temptation: sleep. Reading anything in front of anybody—with the possible exception of the Riot Act—is guaranteed to unlimber yawns and flutter eyelids. The reason is simple. If you, the speaker, seem more interested in your papers than in people, your listeners are tempted to show more concern for the clock than for you.

Clock-watching is almost a clinical definition of boredom. Put yourself in the listeners' pews. When a speaker pays no attention to you, when courtesy forbids you from doing a crossword puzzle or humming Willie Nelson, and you are stuck on a hard wooden chair, time stretches. The guy up there drones along in his singsong. He trips over words. He looks up (if at all) in the wrong places. He revs

up scripted anger, programmed humor. He plows on when
he should flow on. You begin to look for the fire exit. This,
unfortunately, is not overstating matters. It's par for the
course.

It does not follow that every noteless speech is a
rafter-rattler. But the written speech, by lessening hope of
surprise, carries a higher hazard of tiring people.

A second reason a read-to listener dozes is loss of intimacy. When you wing your speech, sermon, pep talk, or
con spiel, your listeners feel a direct bond with you:
mouth-to-ear respiration. You have their attention because
they've got yours. They're flattered; you're listened to.

This intimacy includes an element we've already dug
into: excitement, the risk that you may lose your way, blow
an argument, derail your train of thought. This unavowed
fascination comes into play most of all for the speaker of
high reputation. Unless people come to hear you merely as
groupies, to touch the hem of your toga, they expect you to
perform—and specifically for them, risking your reputation a little by "improvising" something new, or appearing
to rethink old things in a new way before their eyes. If you
don't, the special link the audience hoped to feel with you
is missing. The folks in front might just as well have read
your book, article, or manifesto.

A third reason why listeners flag when you read is that
they lose respect for you. Not only does reading or card-
flipping make them doubt your ability to think on your
feet; it raises ugly suspicions about your expertise, maybe
even about ghost-writers. Since the whole idea of making
a speech is to win your audience, such doubts are bad
news.

And don't count on your crutch-wielding stirring your listeners' sympathy. It will—but as pity for you, not liking for your ideas, if you awake people to those at all.

Add to all this the almost unavoidable stiltedness of a read speech, and you have a patentable solution for insomnia. While your listeners are sleeping, they will dream resentful dreams of you robbing them. Robbing them of attention, of intimacy, of excitement, and of esteem for you.

c) *The Speaker:* If writing speeches tends to constipate eloquence, and drive audiences to counting flies on the ceiling, it can make a good speaker into a robot. Speaking ought to be exciting for you as well as your listeners. Clinging to paper inspiration takes away your best fun in sounding off.

Why? Because a text makes almost impossible the warm, easy, free-flowing communication you want with your audience. As we've often shown, making a satisfying speech is like making love—indeed, you should think of every speech as a seduction. Glueing your eyes to a text on a lectern is like attempting to melt a newfound heart-throb while flipping through the Kama Sutra.

You must try not just a little tenderness. Be subtle. Once you creep into your public's heart, you can then, as one tends to with familiar loves, get both rougher and blunter.

Remember how Groucho Marx charmed his studio audience with easy-nasty banter? Remember how Carol Burnett did the same with easy-gentle repartee? Whatever your temperament and style, you too can subjugate your listeners. The only trick, which is not one because it is truth itself: be yourself. And to be that, you must *be* yourself, not a declaimer of words off a page.

One of the most persuasive media men in North America is René Lévesque. Before and after he became premier of Quebec, Mr. Lévesque displayed a mastery of televised psychology to shrivel with envy his former colleagues in TV public affairs. Mr. Lévesque's formula for moving millions of individuals (a recipe known to most great performers) is to speak quite simply, to *one* individual. Imagine *one* person, preferably a friend or relative (whom, incidentally, you like), and you will transmit warmth and trust enough to conquer the crowd. This nugget of common sense recalls the advice of my radio-producer friend who suggested: "Don't read it; *tell* me about it." The idea is to humanize your mass appeal by making it a personal, one-on-one appeal. Your message almost instinctively becomes a seductor's "line"—not necessarily a dishonest line, just a natural and engaging one. And you, Don Juan or Mata Hari, become the speaker we all love to hear, and if possible even believe.

Another reason reading spooks a speaker is that it stops him from reacting to his audience. Instead of reading a text, a good speaker ought to spend half his effort "reading" his public. (He might devote the other half to deciding what he wants to say. . . .)

Even for a speaker trying to brighten a dreary occasion, it's helpful to keep free and flexible. Then you can "bounce off" an audience's boredom, excitement, anger, laughter, or sadness. This creates a dynamic that brings the hall alive. It sets up between speaker and listeners an intellectual and emotional dialogue.

Examples? You spot five guys in the back row who just fell off their chairs. If they did so with laughter (and you're sure they're laughing with you, not at you), you might unhastily rev up more witticisms like the ones that broke them up. If they fell off because they had fallen asleep, then you know you're in trouble. You had better add some new juice to your flagging oration—maybe by smashing your water glass and bellowing something profoundly superficial like, "Who says there are no simple answers?"

A more dramatic case might be the courtroom lawyer. As Perry Mason would tell you anytime, an on-his-toes attorney needs to scan his jury as a hawk does a mouse, even if a trifle less obviously. Judging how each sally makes or misses its mark, weighing how gut emotion works against dry fact or specious logic, watching how this gesture, that modulation moves the jury members' eyes—all such assessments of signals demand that the advocate stand unencumbered by text. He must be ready to shift his ground, fine-tune his approach, and better target his technique.

Even for a speaker not called on to save his client from the clinker, freedom from the written word can prove precious. Let's not put too fine a point on it: if you discover early in your talk, or halfway through, that you are bombing, not having a text leaves you some chance to salvage a lousy speech.

It's not that you should suddenly take the opposite view to the one you were wiping out with, but you can change your tone or tangent. Instead, say, of denouncing vivisection by drawing tears for suffering animals, you might try a touch of closer-to-home horror by claiming that vets who chop up dogs for research have been known to turn to vampirism on young girls. . . .

Don't kid yourself that you can always slip in a few clever asides to liven up a recited text. "Spontaneous" asides in a written-and-read speech make the same hiccup impact you get from four- by six-inch idiot cards. They stand out like cymbals in a serenade, glaringly reminding your audience that you are an oratorical cripple.

Would you care to test how insidious texts can be in sapping your mental juices? Try a little run at what we shall modestly portray as Spicer's Law:[1] *The more text you have, the more you will use.* Take any simple theme you know well, and give yourself three minutes to speak on it. The first time, write out, and read out, every word of it; the second, speak from idiot cards; the last, jot down a skimpy "Cartesian" outline on the back of a small envelope, then stuff the envelope in your pocket and wing it.

Unless you are the wrong kind of genius, you cannot get lost with your full text; you may waffle a bit on your idiot cards; and you will stumble more elegantly than you imagined with the stuffed-away envelope. Now here's the crunch: go back and try to improvise from the full text. You can't—not without long, choppy pauses while you read a whole written-out thought, then try to restate it. Every time you want to vary or develop this thought, you find yourself asking, in a mixture of panic and curiosity, whether you are missing something on the paper. Or whether it isn't time to refer back to the text to pick up a new thought.

---

1. Still another sneaky variation, of course, on Parkinson's Law.

In all, your attempt to wing it from a fully written text will fail: you keep grabbing at crutches you're afraid you'll misplace. The same holds, to a lesser degree, for the idiot cards: you feel drawn back to them like a nervous magnet, always in search of a security that is only there on its own terms (stop-start eloquence), never on yours (flowing, interestingly paced eloquence).

You will have sensed by now that paper is a two-faced adversary—its "safety" becomes slavery. To fight it, you need a ruthless method: keep paper off your platform. If you don't dominate the paper, it will dominate you—and precisely to the degree that you allow it to. More paper means more bondage for you; less and less paper means you can fly more and more freely. In sum, a written text offers a false security—not really security at all, but entrapment.

The final reason for shucking your notes is good old down-to-earth physiology. To pump out the adrenaline you need to focus your mind, you need a healthy dose of creative terror. Only some fear of failing—the nightmare of losing your place or blanking out in public—is galvanizing enough to push you to your natural summits. In being so pressed, you are likely, with a little training such as we offer here, *not* to get lost or blank out. You will simply speak more pungently. You will change paralyzing tension into stimulating energy.

In letting creative terror open the sluice gates, you will not swim with a life jacket. But after mastering the common-sense tricks taught in Parts One and Two of this book, you will know how to *swim*—with confidence, grace, and as much spontaneity as you can train yourself to squeeze out of that delightful, thought-clarifying terror.

All that goes to say that if you persist in pampering yourself with paper speeches, you will also feel scared, but scared stiff. Some used to claim it was better to be dead than Red. Tell yourself, as you prepare to fly, that whenever you drag a text onstage, you are both read *and* dead.

2. Practice Makes
Fallibly Impressive

If you have really read and soaked up the previous ten chapters, as opposed to glancing at the conclusion to see if this book is worth buying, you should now be an accomplished "improviser." As a graduate of the *Winging It* school of high-flying speech, you can now face fearlessly the many chances that come your way to pontificate in public.

You and I and your fellow graduates know that you are not a different person in character or talents. However, you are something more accessible and useful: a disciplined orator, a thinker and speaker with a method. You may not possess new genius or new energies, but you have learned to invest instead of squander the intellect you have. You know how to channel, not disperse, your ideas and emotions.

When should you start this investing and channeling? Immediately, through an amazing invention called practice. Practice. Need I remind you that all our fun with theory, techniques, and drills is futile without practice? To transform winging it from an exercise in book-browsing into a marrow-deep, instinctive skill, you must decide *now* to leap on as many opportunities, and kinds of opportunities, to speak publicly as you can seize.

Doing so will get you tagged as an egomaniac, but you would not be reading a book like this if you were not a closet one anyway, so let your true personality emerge. Become a mike-grabbing, platform-stealing, telepromptered Cartesian star—today, if not earlier.

Those who come to scoff at your flamboyance will remain to pray—or at least to listen enthralled to you, this foolhardy, formerly average guy or gal who has somehow learned to command a crowd to become a coterie. They will admire you as a magician who can stand up, speak up, and shut up, leaving an audience of two or two thousand with the tingling joy of having been courted and won.

As you sneak or solicit invitations to speak, vanquish residual fears by reminding yourself that you have a secret weapon. You have a method: a reliable, all-purpose technique for taking on any topic, stripping it to the core, reassembling it logically, and presenting it in a clear, persuasive manner. Without notes but not without preparation, you can speak on any subject with poise and spontaneity. Knowing this will jolt you with adrenaline every time you make a speech, or even angle to do one.

Scorn no reasonable chance to open your mouth in public—in class, at a convention, during a union or political meeting, at an in-office round table, or even with your Tupperware or Lovecraft circle. Naturally you should adapt the winging-it method to your audience's size and character: for an intimate group, many of our tricks for delivery, and even preparation, are simply not needed. Be sure, though, to exercise your brain a lot—and soon—on the parts of this book you do need. Winging it, like mental arithmetic, tennis, or romance, follows one inexorable law: if you don't use it, you lose it. We now will send you into the sunset with a final chapter dispensing gloom for the inarticulate others, and glee for smooth-talking you.

An orator is a good man who is skilled in speaking.

—CATO THE ELDER

CHAPTER TWELVE

Broodings After Touchdown

Fasten your seat belts for a brief post-landing lecture. We're going to have a little turbulence here from your pilot instructor—who, you may mutter, must have missed his vocation as an angry priest. Do not plug your ears. This end-of-book meditation could help you do your own fresh thinking about the place eloquence holds in your life and in society. Besides, the angry-priest stuff is really just a set-up for our last few pages of unquibbling uplift.

We'll look first at what's wrong with eloquence in America, then show you how you and I and a few others with TV in our heads are going to make the world safe for demagogy—well, say, for formerly shy speakers.

1. Eloquence in Eclipse

Need I remind you that we live in the Age of Unintelligibility—an era of decline for all the oratorical arts?

(In "oratorical" I include any form of vocal expression except singing: conversation, discussion, debate, lecturing, and hectoring.) Grace, wit, cadence, harmony, simple elegance—of these we hear less and less as more and more people speak in public. Why?

a) *Heart Over Mind:* Today's ideal is no longer cleanly crafted speaking. It is not even the conveying of facts and ideas. It is something like inarticulate sincerity, like mindless self-righteousness. This intellectual pollution spread from the 1960s me-generation, who thought good intentions displaced good ideas.

With their ferocious cult of mediocrity, many egalitarian anarchists suppose that a good speaker is one who gets upset to the point of incoherence. Insult and anger replace eloquence. One measures brilliance not in finely honed argument, but in decibels of the maudlin. One does not think. One *feels.* However, it would be wrong to blame only the fad of a decade for our decadence in speech. Many other factors come into play.

b) *New World Self-consciousness:* Perhaps the first culprit is the laziness and license in speech universal to the New World. Seemingly a perpetual frontier, the forty-odd nations that experiment with English, French, Spanish, or Portuguese in the Western Hemisphere have never lost the taste for coining new words, and even new syntax, which dynamic young societies tolerate. Living languages need to evolve, but you don't have to be a pedant or a purist to refuse to call all loose talk creative. There is lively talk and deadly talk. There is urbane and awkward. There is jerry-built junk talk—like, you know, huh?

Starting with the eighteenth-century myth that good speech was a smokescreen for colonialist manipulations, this reverse snobbery persists in the deliberate hickery of many otherwise intelligent people toward "fancy-talking sharpies." When speakers apologize for precision and imagination, when they tie their own tongues, eloquence is in decline by any standard.

Ain't that true? Nostalgia, as Simone Signoret observed, is not what it used to be.

c) *BOMFOG and Bafflegab:* At all levels of society, eloquence wilts, too, under the assaults of pomposity and evasion, of euphemism, cant, and mumbo-jumbo.

BOMFOG—an invention of the late, lovable Nelson Rockefeller—stands for the Brotherhood of Man under the Fatherhood of God. One of Rockefeller's favorite phrases, it provided journalists with an irreverent acronym to describe almost all of the above vices. Put it under the cold eye of a microscope, and you won't find much in the way of meaning. But does it ever sound good, and does it ever make you feel cozy!

Listen next time to your preferred politician, the one who sends waves of warm feeling flowing over your soul. Analyze his or her exact meaning. Then weep—for the speaker spouting such claptrap, and for yourself, drinking it in. When vulnerable to rhetoric, when craving to be led out of our collective or personal anguish, we are all susceptible to BOMFOG, but if you want to keep control of your country or yourself, ration your binges of BOMFOG. It turns your mind to mush. It turns your homeland into a dictatorship.

Do I exaggerate again? I think not. George Orwell, in his essay "Politics and the English Language," showed how euphemism masks and promotes tyranny. When a statesman caresses you with sweet nothings about "the responsibility of government for the progress and well-being of our interdependent community," slap your wallet and/or run for cover: the guy has his hand in your pocket and/or is planning to tell you when, where, and how you can grow nasturtiums.

What of bafflegab? Or as its leading satirist, James H. Boren of *When In Doubt, Mumble,* calls it, what of "fuzzification"?

By these evocative words we mean the near-universal trend of bureaucrats, politicians, and other power-trip befuddlers to complicate the simple, disguise the limpid, or, more often, hide "facts" that are not there in the first place.

Boren, through his Washington-based National Association of Professional Bureaucrats, Inc. (NATAPROBU) has been leading a one-man guerrilla war on obscurity, obtuseness, and obfuscation. Unlike Britain's Sir Ernest Gowers, whom Winston Churchill named in 1940 to save England by saving English in the Civil Service, Boren makes no appeal, however witty, to restore English as a medium of communication. He baits the enemy bureaucrats through a pseudo-glorifying parody—by ostensibly congratulating them for triumphs in circumlocutory vacuity.

Circumlocutory vacuity? Possibly we mean parameter-extension of impenetrable insignificances or adumbration-analysis of dynamic reality interfaces. You get what we mean.

Alas, alas, such stuff is not far enough from dynamic reality. Read your latest income-tax return or fishing regulations. You will find bureaucratic "truth" stranger than Boren-style fiction.

How can you keep such flatulent double-speak out of your speaking? By a fanatical vigilance for any word or phrase that offends against directness, clarity, or simplicity. By reading a brilliant book called *The Art of Plain Talk*, by Rudolph Flesch.[1] And by practicing, when writing, to chop out ruthlessly all overgrowths of cliché and embroidery.

Two practical tricks. Discipline yourself, when rereading something you've written, to delete automatically any phrase you cannot understand or clarify within two or three minutes. Then start the whole paragraph from scratch until you get it. Or play a game with your editorial machete: pay yourself a fictitious dollar for every word you can cut out of your writing. These games are brutal, but they work.

When you return from spending all those easily won dollars in Monte Carlo, buy yourself a tape recorder with what little is left. Then listen critically to a speech you have winged as an exercise, and stop the machine every time you spot a sample of BOMFOG or bafflegab. You will

1. Rudolph Flesch, *The Art of Plain Talk*, New York, Harper & Row, 1946.

be surprised, horrified, but soon attuned to censoring your junk talk as you speak. Prune your clutter, and you will grow strong and straight-talking.

d) *Television: Mush for the Mind:* A perceptive wag once held that if Beethoven and Einstein had watched, as most North Americans do, twenty-five to thirty-five hours of TV a week, they would have turned out as functional illiterates in their trades. If watching too much TV weakens self-expression and kills conversation, how does performing on TV harm good speaking? In three ways. First, it intimidates most speakers into using either a text, idiot cards or a teleprompter. Knowing you may be reaching a million or more listeners tends to freeze you—to a text, or anything at all on paper.

Second, TV poses a unique problem of deciding who your audience is. If you are speaking to a fairly large audience in a hall, but parts or all of your speech happen to be televised, you face a "two-public" dilemma intrinsic to TV.

Why? Because, as Marshall McLuhan showed, TV is a "cool," calm, intimate medium requiring an easygoing, quiet manner. Addressing a crowd, even with a very good sound system, demands a more commanding presence, a more dramatic, "hot" approach. Should you speak intimately, for one favorite person, as the TV experts advise, to capture the thousands or millions in their living rooms? Or should you zero in on your immediate audience, by striking a more keenly defined figure, by heightening tastefully the pose of your stage persona?

The question is a nice one. It demands a subtle tradeoff of expectations by both speaker and audience. If you need to sway your immediate listeners more than you do your unseen public, you should of course take the more stagy route. If your immediate audience is essentially a foil, a claque, or mere decor for your TV show, plainly you must shade down the theatrics and speak gently to the TV cameras—making love to the lens, as one erotically over-wrought performer not too inaccurately put it.

Your audience in the hall may also influence you by its hopes. Are they counting on you to galvanize the weak-kneed for a crusade against illegible graffiti or to shame the niggardly into mortgaging their homes to finance foster nests for the offspring of unwed parakeets? In such cases, you cannot let them down. Give 'em a barn-burner, and let the cynical eye of the TV camera mock your histrionics. Maybe, if you have some sense of proportion, you won't look *too* silly.

If your audience sees in you a figure with a legitimate audience beyond the hall, they will not hate you for playing to the cameras. Just don't make it too obvious. A little courtesy to your captive audience goes a long way even on TV. The occasional tip of the hat to the hall will win you more marks than unsullied slickness.

If you must be so calculating, tell yourself you are dabbling in studied amateurism. That's so aristocratic.

What do you do when both your audience in the hall and the TV viewers are vital to you? Somehow you must play to both. This task is daunting. As Lance Morrow pointed out in his superb *Time* magazine essay (August 18, 1980) on "The Decline and Fall of Oratory," working both sides of the camera is "an extraordinarily difficult trick." He quotes Republican Congressman Guy Vander

Jagt as describing the two-medium choice as like "having one bullet and having to shoot north and south at the same time."

Subdued drama? Intense calm? Something like that is what you need. Neither shout nor saw the air. Learn to possess yourself onstage, and you will find that your confident, radiant presence, combined with a simple, easily spoken speech, will build you a bridge between your two audiences. As you cross it, don't let playing hot and cold at the same time come off as tepid. Just be honest in your ideas and straightforward in your pitch. With this and luck, you can interest both audiences.

In Morrow's view, two of the best practitioners of the two-medium art are two men with quite different levels of skills: Ronald Reagan and Jimmy Carter. Reagan pulls it off with the polished assurance of decades before face-scanning cameras, plus an economical sense of gesture natural to his "nice guy" personality. Carter, notes Morrow, "also possesses a shrewdly understated style. A Carter speech that seems pale and weak in person comes through coaxial cables giving off just the right small personal glow."

Think of this two-public dilemma next time you are watching a political convention on TV. If the platform speaker is trying to win votes in the hall to claim a nomination as his party's candidate, you will notice how he plays mainly to the crowd—even though most votes are already sewn up. Once he has won the nomination, and must corral votes among the public outside the hall, he will, if he is good, tend to calm down, become more statesmanlike and, above all, more intimate.

The change may not be striking, but it should mirror a different shading: the nuance of leaving the vote-gathering forum of the barnlike hall to enter the cozier ballot booth of your living room.

TV's final dismantlement of structured eloquence comes in its chop-and-chew editing techniques. As a purveyor of thirty- to ninety-second blitzes of visual and "sound" information, TV news demands that speech writers plan short, sharp bursts of quotable copy. Even more than for newspapers and magazines, speakers wishing TV coverage must learn to build a whole speech around a headline—with, as Morrow again points out, "a few key and newsy sentences in oratorical neon to make the networks."

Structure, logic, and finely reasoned argument all fade before this compulsion to encapsulate. A speech aimed at TV becomes a shapeless wandering which sometime, anytime, stumbles onto a made-for-TV newsworthy nugget.

Skilled TV manipulators arrange to tip off reporters about "interesting" passages. Skilled reporters make up their own minds—but still more skilled speakers have been known to sit on their juicy potential TV clip until they spot the video camera's red light go on, or until the film camera's stage-lighting goes on. Then the rascals reach deep into their grab-gab speech and dredge out the passage they want on the TV news. For the TV audience, the speech's coherence and reasoning matter naught. They get to judge only the flickering seconds of airtime.

It's a shoddy little game of smoke and mirrors—but with votes, power, and money at stake, boys will be boys and politicians will be frauds.

Under these three pressures of TV—to read, to split audiences, and to sacrifice all to one zingy quote—eloquence has faded, perhaps fatally. Are orderly argument, spontaneity, and style apart from the flippant doomed?

2. The Ironic Alchemy: Fighting TV's Fire with 'Televised' "Thought on Fire"

Wait. Before you weep for eloquence lost, think back on what you have just read. Then consider this small irony: could not you and I and a few other fans of fine speech counterattack with the enemy's doomsday weapon? Could we not use our imaginary TV screens, Descartes on our mind's-eye teleprompter, to reverse the ravages TV has wrought on eloquence?

The thought is pleasantly presumptuous. The situation is so bad, the decadence of speech so seemingly final, that maybe we should suppress false modesty and give the idea a fling.

To measure how winging it might help, let's recall the elements of eloquence. Then we'll review how winging it can supply some of these. Finally, we'll look at how we might teach the innocent shams of winging it to enough people to start turning the tide of the tongue-tied.

a) *The Elements of Eloquence:* If eloquence, as William Jennings Bryan phrased it, is indeed "thought on fire," where are the thoughts and where are the matches? Most thoughts can be found by starting five, ten, twenty, or thirty years ago, when you got your basic education. If you did not begin with a broad general culture, you ought to start filling in the gaps today. Read widely, but read well. Read the best stuff in all and any fields that pique your fancy. Knowing many fields even superficially gives you the raw materials for comparison and context. Without these, perspective—and intelligence itself—has trouble flowering.

That's for in-depth or background thought. The foreground thoughts you need, the ideas fleshing out your present topic for speaking, must come from homework. Insultingly obvious? Not so. Plenty of people believe that winging it in public proceeds only from instinct, from naked, unpolished talent. That's a foolish error. Talent doesn't hurt, but speaking, like any fine art, rests on training, practice, rehearsal. Never be vain enough to speak thoughtlessly, counting on sheer inborn brilliance to bulldoze you through. In a pinch and for a short while, it can. But unless your reservoir is deep, and the surge of your current strong, your stream will run thin. You will give a shallow speech.

Remember Mark Twain and his three weeks' preparation for an impromptu speech? Prepare, and you will be spontaneous. Tension comes only from being unprepared, and knowing it.

A second element of eloquence, as we have stressed from beginning to end of this book, is a sense of order. Master the technique outlined in *Winging It,* and you will have at least an approach to order. If you can work out your own variations on this, or even your own completely different system, do it—but concern yourself with structure, logic, and the shape of your speaking. Form should, of course, follow content. Raw content, though—undisciplined, unmolded by symmetry and consequence—is nothing but a stream of consciousness. Shrinks go crazy listening to *that*.

A third element is music. Call it cadence or harmony if you wish. Eloquence must ride on waves of rhythm, on sea swells of uplift and down-swoop which leave listeners suspended on your words. Like rocking a baby, the ebb and flow of good speech should cradle the listener until you have lulled him into your movements of mind and style.

Finally, do not forget risk. Fine speaking demands a mood of mystery, an enchanting uncertainty that grips listeners and makes them want to watch. It is the same sense of imminent danger that rivets us to the launching of a space shuttle, to the dancing of a circus gymnast on a tightrope. Never forget to weave into your oratorical spell the unspoken questions: "What will he say next?" and "Can she really keep this up?"

Depth, order, music, suspense: a compelling cocktail. Take a stiff drink of it, and now we'll go on TV.

b) *TV and Telepathy:* How can we throw the trickery of television back in television's teeth? How can we mobilize the visual medium *par excellence* to restore the elements of eloquence to public speaking?

Think back on what you have just learned, and you will see. Seeing is precisely what we have been trying to inject into your speeches: the art of putting pictures in people's heads—beginning with your own.

The winging-it method scripts images in your mind, focuses them in a rational order, then runs them past your mind's-eye on an invisible screen. Rolling our friend Descartes onto an imaginary teleprompter, we have been teaching you how to see in your head each speech or talk as a carefully written and directed TV show.

The magic of this fanciful TV works for your audience too. Because the winging-it technique treats your listeners as a television audience, as rather bored, blasé TV-watchers needing to be seduced away from competing "channels" of daydreaming, it highlights, illustrates, reminds, and reinforces constantly. It tries to make your "show" as easy to watch and listen to as possible. It does so by using a strong, clear structure, sweep-along momentum, colorful pictures, and the daredevil charm of "live" (that is, apparently improvised) TV.

If you think of each presentation you give as a TV show, as a visual as much as an aural exercise, you will instinctively strengthen all these elements of good TV . . . and good eloquence. As in many of the black arts we have discussed in this book, psychology, or stimulative self-delusion, plays a vital part.

Do you fear that psyching yourself up to master these arts of make-believe TV is something artificial? I presume you also dismiss every ballet dancer, sports coach, and suitor as a phony for indulging in limbering up, pep talks, or candlelight and wine.

Almost anything worthwhile gains by first getting yourself in the mood. Ronald Reagan's valiant press secretary, James Brady, insisted plaintively that warming up was par, even for a press conference: "Where," he complained when hit cold with a nasty question at the start of a press breakfast, "has foreplay gone?" Where indeed?

However you work this out with yourself, you should savor this irony of turning TV techniques against TV, the enemy of eloquence. I believe the ideas outlined here merely echo much of the oratorical common sense of the ancients. Demosthenes, Pericles, Cicero, and all their pre-TV disciples knew and used most of *Winging It*'s underpinning. We, TV's benumbed and bedazzled children, mainly are plagiarizing and updating.

Since the time of the last great orators of World War II—Churchill, Roosevelt, and, unfortunately, Hitler—society's ability to nurture and accept masterful speech has withered alarmingly. The causes we listed for the decline of eloquence conspire to make a comeback of fine speech seem impossible. Impoverished English teaching in schools and our new submission to COBOL- and FORTRAN-speaking computers spark no optimism either.

It's because good public speaking could be, so to speak, on its last legs, that our image of television as both assailant and savior is ironic but apt. What fun to believe that we can all become TV stars while making history— legends in our own minds!

c) *Getting the Picture . . . into Everybody's Head:* My God. Are we going to produce a society of prima donnas? That would not be such a bad idea if most of them sought to tutor their talents. If this little handbook manages to turn on a fair number of self-convinced timid people to their inborn potential to speak well, I'll cash my royalty checks unremorsefully.

As a renegade professor, though, I confess grander hopes—perhaps not for this book, but for the cause, the nearly lost cause, of articulateness. I have hopes for the millions of intelligent people, young and old, men and women, who freeze when they are called on to open their mouths in public.

This other kind of "silent majority" represents one of the great losses of talent in our society. Intelligence and wisdom do little good (apart from their virtue being their own delightful reward) if they are trapped inside a sluggish tongue. The tongue, of course, is not the real culprit. The deeper source of muddled speech is muddled thinking. It is lack of a philosophical framework. It is inability to channel free-flowing genius through a focusing structure. It is, ultimately, the failure to remember the age-old lesson known to all successful artists: freedom emerges from order.

In recalling this, I know I am riding solidly in the saddle behind Don Quixote. Convincing hundreds of thousands of school administrators and teachers that you teach freedom through discipline is tilting at windbags. As long as the mentors of our youth prefer to preach in BOMFOG and bafflegab about letting the kids' intellectual water flow to its own level, it will: to the lowest.

Maybe we, the escapees from school, can lead the children's crusade. If you are free from the academic free-for-all, if you are out in the world and able to captain your destiny, start to work on getting the oratorical best from yourself, and giving it.

Infect a few friends within your group or organization to leash, then loosen, their tongues. Break all tradition and chat thoughtfully with your spouse, lover, or family at table. Above all, seek every chance to risk your reputation. Do this not by talking nonsense, but by daring to speak wisdom—wisdom reshaped by your own one-of-a-kind mind and heart.

Now you've understood, mastered, and digested the mysteries of winging it. What well-wishing words might launch you on your way?

Stretch the wings we've glued on you, you latter-day Icarus of eloquence. Beware the sun, but poise to soar as high as you can.

Then climb a cliff and fly.